New

VE

GW01003411

Absolute Press

New
VEGETARIAN
Cuisine

A second collection of favourite recipes from the
leading vegetarian restaurants in Great Britain

Published by Absolute Press (Publishers)
14 Widcombe Crescent, Widcombe Hill, Bath, Avon
BA2 6AH. (0225) 316013

First published November 1986

© Absolute Press (Publishers)

Editor and Compiler Paula Borton
Cookery Editor Jenny Scopes

Illustrations
Joe Mallia

Cover printed by
Stopside, Unit 6, Stable Yard,
Windsor Bridge Road, Bath

Text photoset by
Quadraset Ltd, E2–3 Second Avenue,
Westfield Industrial Estate,
Midsomer Norton, Bath, Avon

Text printed by
WBC Print, Barton Manor, St. Philips, Bristol

Bound by
WBC Bookbinders, Maesteg

Contents

Introduction

When New Vegetarian Cuisine's predecessor, Vegetarian Cuisine, was first published in 1982 it proved an instant success. Somehow the simple formula of salads, starters, main dishes and sweets, simply laid out in an uncomplicated and accessible style, caught the culinary imaginations of vegetarians and non-vegetarians alike. The strength in depth of Britain's vegetarian restaurant chefs ensured a collection of recipes covering all aspects and influences of vegetarian cooking. Four years on, with the standards of excellence ever rising, the formula has been repeated in the confident expectation that it will prove just as popular.

Once again the recipes have been assembled into the four main categories — starters, salads, main dishes and sweets — and once again there is no pretence that the collection of wonderfully eclectic recipes offers anything approaching a balanced nutritional regime. These are recipes to be enjoyed! Superb dishes, whose origins and influences span the culinary world, from China to Mexico, Japan to Hungary, from east to west and south to north.

This book would not have been possible without the support and enthusiasm of the many vegetarian chefs who so generously and willingly gave of their time and expertise — and of course their recipes. New Vegetarian Cuisine is a tribute to their skills and dedication.

Salads

Alfalfa and Orange Salad

Neal's Yard Bakery, London
Chef; Rachel Haigh

4 oz (125g) alfalfa sprouts
2–3 oranges, peeled, segmented and chopped
1 tablespoon sesame seeds

For the dressing:

4 tablespoons soya or sunflower oil
1 tablespoon cider vinegar
1 teaspoon soya sauce

Tease the sprouts apart, or if necessary, roughly chop them. Add them to the oranges and sesame seeds.

Mix all the dressing ingredients together well.

Just before serving pour the dressing over the salad and toss.

Apple and Celery with Almond and Tahini Dressing

Everyman Bistro, Liverpool

9 oz (250g) crisp apples, well washed
French dressing
½ head celery (9 oz/250g) trimmed and washed
2 tablespoons tahini sauce
4 fl oz (125ml) natural yoghurt
salt and pepper to taste
2 oz (50g) flaked almonds

A lighter, modern version of the maitre d's creation at the Waldorf-Astoria. He was fond of saying "my job is the serving of food, never the cooking". Well, maybe his head chef should have said, "I think that salad would be better done this way".

Core the apples and cut them into small chunks, dropping them immediately into the French dressing.

Cut the celery sticks into ½" (1cm) sections and place them in a mixing bowl. Add the tahini and yoghurt, mix well and season to taste with salt and pepper.

Thoroughly drain the apple chunks, add them to the dressed celery and again mix well. Fold in most of the flaked almonds and turn into a serving dish, decorating the top with the reserved almonds.

Arame and Carrot Salad

Wild Oats II, Bristol
Chef; Sarah Wale

14 oz (400g) carrot, grated
14 oz (400g) onion, finely chopped
1 tablespoon sunflower oil
2 oz (50g) sunflower seeds
½ oz (15g) dried arame sea vegetable
shoyu to taste

Sweat the onion and carrot in the oil until they release their juices – about 20 minutes.

Dry roast the sunflower seeds.

Cook the arame in about ¼ pint (150ml) water until all the water has been absorbed.

Leave all the ingredients to cool.

Mix everything together well, adding shoyu to taste, and serve.

Butter Bean Salad

Quarry Shop, Machynlleth
Chef; Anne Lowmass

8 oz (225g) butter beans
1 onion
4 tomatoes
sprig of fresh mint or a sprinkle of dried mint

For the dressing:

½ pint (275ml) sunflower oil
¼ pint (150ml) cider vinegar
pinch dry mustard
1 teaspoon honey
1 clove garlic, crushed
pinch ground black pepper

Cook beans for about an hour or until tender, strain and leave to cool. (Soak the beans first if possible to save on the cooking time.) Don't overcook the beans or the salad will become mushy!

Chop onion finely and quarter or slice the tomatoes. Chop mint if fresh.

Mix all the dressing ingredients together until well blended and pour over the salad just before serving.

Garnish with a sprig of mint.

Spicy Bulgar Salad

Huckleberry's, Bath
Chef; Katy Beauchamp

3 cups bulgar wheat
1 teaspoon curry powder
1 teaspoon turmeric
1 teaspoon paprika
¾ cup sweetcorn
¾ cup diced carrot
¾ cup diced banana soaked in lemon juice
¾ cup peanuts, roasted for 20 minutes and then covered with ¼ cup tamari
    when hot
¾ cup dried mixed fruit
1 tablespoon soya oil

Place the bulgar in a saucepan and add enough boiling water to just cover it. Cover tightly and leave for 15 minutes to cool. At the end of this time the wheat should have absorbed all the water. Leave to go completely cold.

Mix all the remaining ingredients into the wheat until they are evenly distributed and serve.

Brussel Sprouts, Orange and Watercress Salad

Henderson's Salad Table, Edinburgh
Chef; Jane McCrone

1 lb (450g) Brussel sprouts
6 oranges
3 bunches watercress
½ pint (275ml) French dressing made with olive oil and lemon juice

Prepare the sprouts, and cut any large ones in half. Blanch in boiling water until just tender. Refresh in cold water.

Peel the oranges and cut the segments into pieces 1" (2cm) long.

Wash the watercress and break it up.

Mix all the ingredients together in a large bowl and toss in the dressing.

Bean Sprout, Melon and Ginger Salad

Delany's, Shrewsbury

1 large carton bought bean sprouts or home-grown (see below)
1 melon, cut the flesh into 1″ (2½cm) cubes
2″ (5cm) root ginger, peeled and grated
juice ½ lemon
French dressing

Bean sprouts take about 3–4 days to do yourself, depending on what type of beans are used. In a large glass jar put about 2″ (5cm) of beans (mung, aduki, whole lentils)—try out different types each time. Cover with water and soak for 24 hours. Cover the top of the jar with muslin so that the jar can be laid on its side to drain. Wash the beans thoroughly each day. Within 4 days the beans will have sprouted. When they are about 1″–1½″ (2–3cm) long they are ready to use and at their most nutritious.

Place the washed bean sprouts in a bowl with the melon and grated ginger. Pour over the lemon juice and French dressing and mix.

This salad can have infinite variety by changing the combination of fruit and sprouts. Nectarines and grapes are particularly good fruits to use.

11

Bean Sprout and Apple Salad

Saxon's, Brighton
Chef; Saxon Howard

½ onion
1 red pepper
2 red-skinned eating apples
4 oz (125g) mung bean sprouts
4 oz (125g) green lentil sprouts
salt and black pepper

For the dressing:

2 tablespoons sour cream
2 tablespoons mayonnaise
2 tablespoons vinaigrette
1 teaspoon tarragon
1 teaspoon chives
2 cloves garlic, crushed
½ teaspoon paprika

Peel and slice the onion very finely. De-seed the pepper and slice into strips. Core the apples and dice them. Mix them all together with the bean sprouts.

Make the dressing by stirring all the ingredients together. Pour over the bean sprout mixture and season to taste with salt and pepper.

Bean Salad

Pilgrims, Tunbridge Wells
Chef; Ann Tolputt

8 oz (225g) cooked kidney beans
8 oz (225g) cooked butter beans
1 red pepper, finely chopped
3 spring onions, finely chopped
oil and vinegar dressing, 2 tablespoons, or more to taste
chopped parsley

Mix all the vegetables together. Pour over the dressing and place in a serving dish.

Just before serving toss the salad and sprinkle over the chopped parsley.

Caribbean Rice Salad

Wholemeal Café, London
Chef; Celia Hide

2 medium bananas
1 small green pepper
1 small red pepper
8 oz (225g) cooked, cold, brown rice
2 oz (50g) roasted peanuts
2 oz (50g) roasted hazelnuts
2 oz (50g) sultanas
3 oz (75g) sweetcorn

Chop the bananas and peppers.

Mix all the ingredients into the rice and stir well.

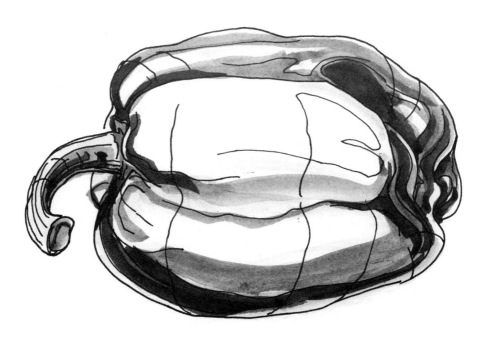

Spicy Carrot and Apple Salad

Cherry Orchard, London
Chef; Linda Campbell

1 ½ lb (900g) carrots
¼ teaspoon cinnamon
½ teaspoon cumin
⅛ teaspoon paprika
¼ teaspoon cayenne pepper
⅛ teaspoon sugar
½ teaspoon salt
1 fl oz (25ml) wine vinegar
1 fl oz (25ml) lemon juice
2½ fl oz (65ml) oil (soya, olive or good vegetable oil)
1 lb (450g) apples (preferably cooking apples)

Top and tail the carrots. Slice them, then either steam or boil until just cooked. Do not let them overcook.

Mix together the spices, lemon, vinegar and oil.

Chop the apple into small chunks.

Mix everything together, preferably while the carrots are still warm. Leave an hour or so before serving to allow the flavours to blend. Serve decorated with chopped parsley.

Cashew Nut, Celery and Vegetable Salad and Gin and Juniper Berry Mayonnaise

Herbs, Coventry
Chef; Robert Jackson

4 oz (125g) cashew nuts
4 oz (125g) celery, finely chopped
2 oz (50g) mushrooms, sliced
1 carrot, grated
½ green pepper, diced
½ red pepper, diced
1 dessertspoon chopped parsley
4 tablespoons mayonnaise
1 tablespoon gin
1 dessertspoon juniper berries, crushed
salt and pepper

Combine together all the dry ingredients.

Combine the mayonnaise, gin and juniper berries together thoroughly.

Dress the salad with the mayonnaise and season to taste.

Cauliflower Salad

Cheese Press, Crickhowell
Chef; Mrs. Morgan-Grenville

1 medium sized cauliflower, divided into small florets
2 carrots, coarsely grated
2 apples, cored and sliced
3 oz (75g) sultanas
1 red pepper, chopped
3 sticks celery, chopped
1 tablespoon freshly chopped chives
1 tablespoon freshly chopped parsley
1 tablespoon lemon juice

For the dressing:

6 tablespoons natural yoghurt
6 tablespoons mayonnaise
1 teaspoon curry paste
salt and black pepper

Mix all the fruit, vegetables and herbs together in a large bowl.

Combine all the dressing ingredients and mix to a smooth cream. Taste and add a little more curry or seasoning if you like. This dressing improves with keeping, so if you can make it 24 hours in advance the curry flavour will intensify.

Pour the dressing over the salad and gently toss until evenly distributed. Mix again just before serving.

Nut Buttered Cauliflower Salad

Serves 4–6

Rainbow's End, Glastonbury
Chef; Shelagh Spear

1 medium sized cauliflower

For the dressing:

2 generous tablespoons crunchy peanut butter
2 tablespoons vegetable oil
lemon juice and salt to taste
½ fresh pineapple, with skin trimmed off (or 1 tin pineapple pieces)
1 sliced red skinned eating apple
1 sliced banana
a few grapes, halved and pipped

Cut the cauliflower into bite-sized florets, rinse and drain in a colander. Reserve some of the pale green leaves to decorate the serving dish.

In a large bowl prepare the dressing by mixing the nut butter and oil and adding a little lemon juice and salt.

Add the fruit to the dressing to avoid any discoloration but save some for decoration. If fresh pineapple is unavailable use a tin of pineapple pieces drained of natural juice (the cook has normaly worked up such a thirst at this stage that the juice provides a welcome drink!). The choice and quantity of fruits used is optional but the sharp tasting fruits like pineapple and apple contrast nicely with the richness of the nut dressing.

Add the cauliflower to the fruit and mix everything together without mashing the fruit.

Pile into a salad bowl or plate lined with cauliflower leaves. Decorate with the reserved fruits.

Celeriac Salad

Guild Café, Bristol

Two large celeriac
salt and pepper

For the dressing:

2 heaped tablespoons good mayonnaise (preferably home-made)
4 heaped teaspoons "grainy" mustard (meaux style)
juice of one lemon
mustard cress or chopped parsley

We find most of our customers are unfamiliar with celeriac. Once the thick, knobbly (and usually very muddy) skin has been hacked off it is a very versatile vegetable. It makes a delicious creamy soup and can be grated like a carrot and added to salads. The following simple recipe using cooked celeriac makes a tasty and unusual alternative to the traditional potato salad.

Peel, chop and cook the celeriac just as if they were potatoes in boiling salted water for about 15 minutes until they are tender.

Drain very thoroughly and chop into smaller cubes. Season while still hot then toss in the dressing.

To make the dressing just mix the mayonnaise, mustard and lemon juice until they are evenly blended.

Toss the celeriac in the dressing, leave to cool and then garnish it liberally with the mustard cress or parsley. Diced cooked carrot can also be mixed in if wished.

Chicory and Watercress Salad

Food For Thought, London
Chef; David Biddulph

chicory
4 oz (125g) bean sprouts
3 heads celery
1 bunch watercress
2 oz (50g) brown almonds
½ cup good vegetable oil and a little lemon juice
1 tablespoon tamari
freshly milled pepper and a pinch salt

Remove the root and blemished leaves of chicory.

Remove the stems from the watercress.

Carefully chop the celery.

Combine the salad vegetables.

Brush the almonds lightly with a little tamari and toast for 15 minutes. Cool.

Mix the oil, tamari and lemon juice, salt and pepper and pour over the salad vegetables and almonds.

Fruit Coleslaw

Good Earth, Wells
Chef; Tina Dearling

1 small white cabbage
1 eating apple
1 pear
1 peach
2 tomatoes
1 banana
1 box cress
2 oz (50g) chopped walnuts

For the mayonnaise:

2 whole eggs
½ level teaspoon dry English mustard
good pinch salt
½ teaspoon muscovado sugar
4 tablespoons vinegar
½ pint (275ml) soya oil

Shred the cabbage finely. Wash all the fruit and cut up into chunks. Peel and chop the banana. Cut the cress and place in a bowl with all the fruit and vegetables and the walnuts.

Make the mayonnaise. Place all the ingredients except the oil in a liquidiser. Turn on and gradually dribble the oil into it. The mixture should thicken up nicely. If it should not thicken up, tip the mayonnaise out of the liquidiser, place another whole egg in the goblet and turn on. Pour the mayonnaise in slowly and it should now begin to thicken.

Add enough mayonnaise to the salad to coat all the ingredients. You may not need all the mayonnaise but it does keep in the fridge for about 2 weeks.

Five Colour Salad with Japanese White Dressing

Everyman Bistro, Liverpool

For the dressing:

5 oz (150g) beancurd, pressed
2 tablespoons sesame seeds
2 teaspoons white sugar
2 teaspoons cider vinegar
½ teaspoon salt
4 oz (125g) white radish, peeled and cut into matchsticks
½ medium carrot, peeled and sliced into thin rounds
4 oz (125g) green beans, topped, tailed and strung if necessary
2 oz (50g) button mushrooms, halved
2 oz (50g) whole sun-dried apricots, washed and finely chopped
grated rind of one lemon, to garnish

Five colour salad combines different colours, shapes, tastes and textures in both a delicious and healthy way. Serve it as a starter or as an accompaniment to other dishes. As a side-dish, five colour salad is particularly good with spicy hot dishes when its cooling flavour is much appreciated.

Prepare the dressing. Mash the pressed beancurd in a bowl. Dry roast the sesame seeds until they brown and start to jump. Crush the seeds into a paste with a pestle and mortar and stir the paste into the mashed beancurd. Stir in the sugar, vinegar and salt until the dressing is of a smooth consistency (or use a blender with a small bowl).

Parboil the radish and carrots in lightly salted water for just 2 minutes each. Drain, and rinse immediately in cold water. Drain again and set aside. Parboil the beans for 3 minutes. Drain, rinse immediately under cold water. Drain again and set aside.

Very lightly sauté the mushrooms in a pan rubbed with vegetable oil.

Combine the vegetables, mushrooms and chopped apricots and stir in the white dressing. Toss to coat all the ingredients. Serve the salad in the centre of individual white plates and garnish with grated lemon rind.

"Bunch of Grapes" Salad

Food for Health, London
Chef; Nolan and Rosemary Highton

For each person you will need:

2 oz (50g) blue cheese (Danish blue, Stilton, Roquefort etc)
2 oz (50g) cream or curd cheese
salt and freshly ground black pepper
plain yoghurt
3–4 oz (75–125g) grapes, black or green (depends on the size of the pears)
½ ripe dessert pear
lettuce, washed, drained and dried
watercress, washed, drained and dried

Place the cheese and seasonings in a blender and blend. If the mixture is very stiff add a little yoghurt, enough to make a smooth, spreading paste. Taste and season. If you are making this for 1–2 people it is easier to do this with a fork or a potato masher in a flat bottomed bowl.

Wash the grapes, cut in half and remove the pips.

Wash the pear, cut in half along the length of the fruit, take out the core with the tip of a teaspoon. Pat the skin dry. Line a small plate with lettuce.

Cover the skin side of the pear with the cheese mixture, using enough to give a secure bedding for the grape halves. Arrange the grape halves on the cheese so that the covered pear looks like a bunch of grapes.

Place the pear on the lettuce and place a small bunch of watercress at the top.

Use two pear halves per person for a larger salad, or surround the pear with small amounts of raw grated salad and hand a dressing separately.

Hazelnut and Sesame Seed Salad

Nature's Way, Eastbourne
Chefs; Dorothy and Maurice Fossitt

12 oz (350g) coarsley grated carrots
6 oz (175g) whole hazelnuts
2 oz (50g) raisins
2 oz (50g) chopped dates
2 oz (50g) sesame seeds
vinaigrette dressing

Mix together the carrots, hazelnuts, raisins, dates and half the sesame seeds.

Add a light dressing of vinaigrette and sprinkle the remaining seeds on top.

Serve on a bed of lettuce or Chinese leaves.

Lima Bean Salad

Hockneys, Croydon
Chef; Paul Keeler

7 oz (200g) lima (butter) beans, soaked overnight
1 dessertspoon turmeric
1 tablespoon vinegar
1 bunch watercress, chopped
1 punnet mustard cress
1 oz (25g) parsley, finely chopped
½ small onion, finely chopped

For the dressing:

8 oz (225g) curd cheese
3 tablespoons wine vinegar
6 tablespoons olive oil
1 tablespoon soft brown sugar

Drain the lima beans and place in a pan of water with the turmeric and vinegar. Cook until tender. Add a little salt near the end of the cooking time.

Drain and refresh the beans and place in a bowl with the watercress, mustard cress, parsley and onion.

Make the dressing by liquidising all the ingredients together.

Pour the dressing over the salad and toss.

Brown Lentil and Rice Salad with Dates and Pumpkin Seeds

Hannah's, Worthing

8 oz (225g) brown rice
8 oz (225g) continental brown lentils, carefully washed
2 oz (50g) dates, chopped
1 oz (25g) pumpkin seeds
1 teaspoon turmeric seeds
1 tablespoon olive oil

This dish is served as a salad at Hannah's but is just as delicious served hot as a main dish. If you prefer, substitute any other dried fruit and seeds for the dates and pumpkin seeds.

Place the rice in a pan of water, add the turmeric and boil for about 30 minutes until the rice is still slightly firm and each grain is separate. Drain and rinse in cold water.

Place lentils in a pan of water and boil for about 40 minutes, until tender. Drain and rinse in cold water.

Mix the lentils and rice together in a bowl, add the remaining ingredients, stir well and serve.

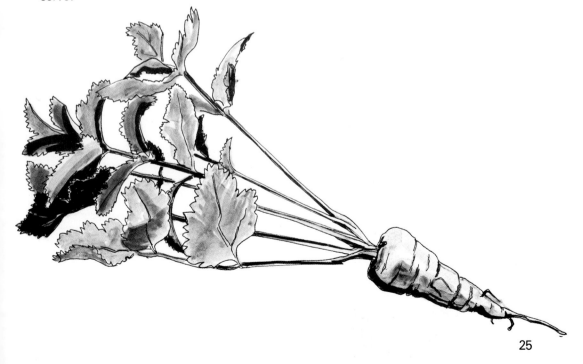

Spiced Potato Salad with Fresh Coriander Leaves

Everyman Bistro, Liverpool

1 ½ lb (700g) potatoes, peeled and grated, or use small, whole new potatoes,
   washed
2 tablespoons sesame seed oil or other vegetable oil
2 oz (50g) sesame seeds
1 tablespoon mustard seeds
1" (2.5cm) fresh root ginger, peeled and finely grated
½ teaspoon chilli powder or hot pepper sauce
salt to taste
juice ½ lemon
2 tablespoons fresh coriander leaves, chopped

Put the potatoes in a pan with plenty of boiling water and boil them until only just
tender. Remove from the heat, drain and put into a salad bowl.

Heat the oil in a frying pan and stir in the sesame seeds, mustard seeds, ginger, chilli
and salt to taste. Fry and stir over a moderate heat for 3–4 minutes.

Stir the oil and spices into the potatoes, add the lemon juice and mix well. Allow to
cool completely and then gently stir in the coriander leaves. Serve or reserve for later
use.

Potato Salad

Herbs, Skipton
Chef; Robert Jackson

1 lb (450g) new potatoes
5 fl oz (150ml) French dressing
1 bunch spring onions, finely sliced
1 tablespoon freshly chopped mint

Boil the potatoes in their skins until tender. Cut into even sized cubes and pour over the French dressing while they are still warm. Leave to cool.

Sprinkle over the spring onions and mint and toss just before serving.

Hot Pasta Salad

Arnolfini, Bristol

12–14 oz (350–400g) spaghetti
6–8 oz (175–225g) grated cheese
6–8 oz (175–225g) black olives, stoned
5 fl oz (150ml) French dressing

Cook the spaghetti in the normal way. Rinse with boiling water.

Stir in the grated cheese, olives and dressing, and serve immediately.

Hedgerow Pasta Salad

Lakeland Hedgerow, Bowness on Windermere
Chefs; Jennifer Mason and Stephen Davy

8 oz (225g) cooked wholewheat pasta spirals
small can of sweetcorn
1 large red pepper, chopped
3 oz (75g) toasted cashew nuts
1 tablespoon lemon juice
salt and pepper
mayonnaise to mix
paprika, for garnish

Combine all the ingredients in a large bowl, using enough mayonnaise to coat thinly.

Place in a serving dish, sprinkle over the paprika. Serve with lemon wedges and watercress.

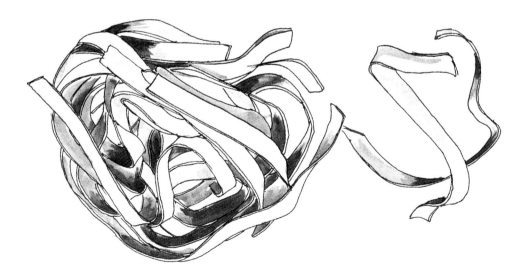

Curried Rice Salad

Marno's, Ipswich
Chef; Penny

6 oz (175g) brown rice
1 medium onion, chopped
3 tablespoons vegetable oil
4 oz (125g) mushrooms, sliced
1 level dessertspoon curry powder
1 tablespoon chutney, preferably mango
juice ½ lemon
1 teaspoon concentrated apple juice
2 tablespoons seedless raisins
4 whole dried apricots, coarsely chopped
2 oz (50g) toasted sunflower seeds

Cook the rice until tender in plenty of water.

While the rice is cooking, gently fry the onion in oil until soft, then add the sliced mushrooms and continue cooking until the slices go limp. Do not overcook. Add the curry powder and cook for another minute, to get rid of the raw flavour, then stir in the chutney, lemon juice, apple concentrate and dried fruit.

Remove from the heat and add the hot, drained rice, mixing well. Leave to cool.

Once cooled, stir in the sunflower seeds, reserving a few to sprinkle over the top as a garnish.

Rice Salad

The Old Bakehouse, Castle Cary
Chef; Carol Seeley

4 oz (125g) cooked short grain brown rice
2 oz (50g) raw button mushrooms
1 oz (25g) flaked almonds
1 dessertspoon sunflower oil
2 cardamom pods — ground in a pestle and mortar

Chop the mushrooms and mix with all the other ingredients. Season to taste.

You can also add a finely chopped green pepper or cucumber and a handful of sultanas — the permutations are endless!

Spinach Salad

Harvest Vegetarian, Ambleside
Chef; Gillian Kelly

1 lb (450g) crisp young spinach
2 oz (50g) sunflower seeds
3 hardboiled eggs

For the dressing:

2 tablespoons olive oil
1 lemon, juiced
2 cloves garlic, crushed
pinch of basil

Remove any tough stems from the spinach, then wash thoroughly. Dry well in a clean tea towel or on kitchen paper, then break up into a bowl.

Dry roast the sunflower seeds until golden brown. Allow to cool for a few minutes then add to the spinach.

Mix all the dressing ingredients together, pour over the spinach and toss.

Sprinkle the top of the salad with diced hardboiled egg.

Spicy Tofu Salad

Cooks Delight, Berkhamsted
Chef; Khaieng Tyler

10 oz (275g) firm tofu
12 oz (350g) mung bean sprouts
½ cucumber
sea salt
1 clove garlic, chopped finely
1 fresh chilli, chopped finely
1 onion, chopped finely
4 oz (125g) unbleached sesame seeds
1 tablespoon unrefined sesame oil
1 tablespoon muscovado sugar
6 tablespoons brown rice vinegar
8 tablespoons filtered water

Cut the tofu into matchstick strips, blanch and drain. Wash bean sprouts, blanch and drain. Cut cucumber into matchsticks and rub ½ teaspoon sea salt into them. Set aside for 10 minutes and drain away the excess water.

Wash sesame seeds, drain and dry roast until aromatic but not burnt!

Heat the oil in a saucepan, add the garlic, chilli and onion and fry for a minute. Add the muscovado sugar and then the rice vinegar and water. Cook for 5 minutes. Add the sesame seeds.

Place the tofu, bean sprouts and cucumber together in a dish and pour the sauce over. Serve immediately.

Wholewheat Salad

Gannets, Newark
Chef; Hilary Bower

1 cup wholewheat
½ cucumber, diced
bunch of radish, sliced into rings
bunch of spring onions, finely sliced
1 tablespoon parsley, roughly chopped
2 oz (50g) walnuts, roughly chopped

For the dressing:

4 tablespoons olive oil (or walnut oil, if available)
2 tablespoons white wine vinegar
1 teaspoon good quality mustard
1 clove garlic, crushed
salt and pepper

Cook the wholewheat in unsalted water for 15–20 minutes at simmering point.
N.B. When cooked, the wholewheat should be "nutty" and not too soft. Drain, and rinse in cold water. Leave to cool.

Add all the other salad ingredients to the wheat and mix well.

Put all the dressing ingredients in a container with a tight fitting lid and shake well. Add to the wholewheat salad and mix well.

# Starters

Broccoli Soup

Serves 6–8

Henderson's Salad Table, Edinburgh
Chef; Ian Wilson

1 medium onion, sliced
2 tablespoons oil
pinch of tarragon
salt and pepper
2 large potatoes, peeled and diced
3 pints (1½ litres) vegetable stock
1½ lb (700g) broccoli, cut into 2″ (5cm) lengths
6 oz (175g) Scottish cheddar or Dunlop, grated
chopped parsley

Fry the onion in the oil until soft. Add the tarragon, salt and pepper, and cook for a little longer before adding the potatoes and half the stock. Cover the pan, and leave to simmer for 10 minutes, stirring occasionally.

Add the remaining stock with the broccoli and simmer until the potatoes begin to break up. Liquidise the mixture and return it to a clean pan. Check the seasoning, re-heat and stir the grated cheese in just before serving. Garnish each portion with a little chopped parsley.

Butter Bean Soup

Serves 6

Cheese Press, Crickhowell
Chef; Mrs Morgan-Grenville

8 oz (225g) butter beans, soaked overnight
1 bay leaf
2 oz (50g) butter
1 onion, finely chopped
2 carrots, finely chopped
1 lb (450g) potatoes, cubed
1 lb (450g) fresh tomatoes, skinned and chopped
basil, to taste
1 vegetable stock cube
salt and pepper
lemon juice, to taste

Boil the butter beans in 2 pints (generous litre) water to which a bayleaf has been added, for about 1¼ hours, until tender but not mushy. Strain, retaining the cooking water.

Melt the butter in a large pan and fry the onion until soft. Add the carrot and potatoes and cook over a gentle heat for ten minutes, stirring occasionally.

Add the tomatoes, beans and then the cooking liquid. Finally stir in the basil and the stock cube and season.

Simmer until all the vegetables are soft, adding a little more water if necessary. Test for seasoning and add a little lemon juice.

Cabbage and Walnut Soup

Serves 4

Cooks Delight, Berkhamsted
Chef; Khaieng Tyler

6 oz (175g) cabbage (either green or white, but not red)
8 oz (225g) organic potatoes
1 teaspoon fresh chervil
1 teaspoon fresh thyme
3 oz (75g) onion
3 oz (75g) best quality walnuts (preferably Hungarian)
2 pints (generous litre) filtered water (or spring water)

salt and pepper
chopped parsley (optional)

Prepare the vegetables. Cut the cabbage into ½" (1cm) squares. Dice the potatoes into ½" (1cm) cubes. Mince the chervil and thyme. Chop the onions finely.

Wash and drain the walnuts, then roast them in the oven until they are crisp and finally chop them.

Warm a saucepan, add the onions and dry fry them for a few seconds. Add the potatoes and cabbage, stir for a few seconds then add ½ pint (150ml) water. Bring to the boil, add the herbs, stir and then add the remaining water. Bring back to the boil, add salt and pepper to taste and leave to simmer for 20 minutes. Garnish with the roasted walnuts. If using white cabbage add some chopped parsley at the end of cooking to enhance the colour.

Carrot and Orange Soup

Serves 6

The Old Bakehouse, Castle Cary
Chef; Carol Seeley

1 ½ lb (700g) carrots
1 large onion
1 large potato
1 sweet and juicy orange
2 oz (50g) Vitaquell or butter
salt
slices of orange, to decorate

Roughly chop the vegetables.

Melt the Vitaquell or butter in a heavy saucepan and fry the onion, potato and carrots gently for a few minutes. Add the orange whole to the pan and cover the vegetables with water. Bring to the boil then lower the heat and simmer until all the ingredients are soft.

Remove the orange and liquidise the vegetables to a smooth consistency.

Return the soup to the pan and add the juice of the orange. Season and adjust consistency of the soup with extra water if necessary. Bring to the boil.

Serve decorated with slices of fresh orange.

Cream of Chestnut Soup

Arnolfini, Bristol

1 large onion, sliced
1 tablespoon oil
2 sticks celery, sliced
2 carrots, chopped
1 bouquet garni
2 pints (1 litre) vegetable stock
14 oz (400g) tin of unsweetened chestnut purée
5 fl oz (150ml) single cream
5 fl oz (150ml) dry sherry

Fry the onion in the oil until golden.

Add the celery, carrots and bouquet garni. Stir in the stock and gradually add the chestnut purée. Bring to the boil and then simmer for 30 minutes.

Remove the bouquet garni and allow to cool slightly before blending in a liquidiser.

Re-heat and stir in the cream and sherry just before serving.

Courgette and Fennel Soup

Herbs, Skipton
Chef; Joan Fikkert

4 oz (125g) onion, sliced
1 clove garlic, crushed
2 oz (50g) butter
1½ lb (700g) courgettes, sliced
1½ pints (900ml) stock
1 teaspoon fennel seeds
5 fl oz (150ml) cream
salt and pepper

Marrows may be used instead of courgettes but they must be peeled and seeded.

Fry the sliced onions and garlic in the butter until transparent.

Add the courgettes and stock and cook for 20 minutes.

Simmer the fennel seeds in a little water, then strain and add to the soup. Season with salt and pepper.

Liquidise the soup and return to a clean pan.

Add the cream, taste for seasoning and gradually re-heat taking care not to bring the soup to the boil after the addition of the cream.

Courgette and Sweetcorn Soup

Serves 4

Harvest Vegetarian, Ambleside
Chef; Gillian Kelly

3 medium courgettes, diced into very small pieces
1 large onion, finely chopped
oil
salt and pepper
1 teaspoon dried chopped chives
1 heaped tablespoon wheatmeal flour
1 pint (575ml) milk
8 oz (225g) packet frozen sweetcorn
shoyu or tamari to taste (optional)

Sauté the courgettes and onion in a little oil until tender. Season with salt, pepper and chives then stir in the flour. Gradually stir in the milk, and stirring continuously, bring the soup to the boil. Leave to simmer gently.

Cook the sweetcorn for a few minutes in boiling, salted water as instructed on the packet. Drain and add to the soup.

Taste for seasoning, adding a splash of shoyu or tamari if desired, a couple of minutes before serving.

Calypso Lentil Soup

Herbs, Coventry
Chef; Robert Jackson

4 oz (125g) red split lentils
1 medium onion
1 medium carrot
4 sticks celery
1 medium red pepper
2 tablespoons vegetable oil
¼ teaspoon chilli powder
¼ teaspoon ground ginger
¼ teaspoon grated nutmeg
2 oz (50g) coconut, desiccated or creamed
1 pint (575ml) water
½ pint (275ml) milk
1 vegetable stock cube
1 tablespoon tomato purée
salt and black pepper

A wonderful spiced lentil soup thick with coconut.

Pour hot water over the lentils and leave for 10 minutes to drain.

Roughly chop all the vegetables.

Heat the oil in a large saucepan, add the vegetables and cook for 4 minutes. Add the spices and cook for a further 2 minutes.

Add the lentils to the pan and stir well.

Add the coconut (if using creamed, break it up first) followed by the water, milk, stock cube and tomato purée. Bring to the boil and simmer for about 50 minutes.

Finally, liquidise or pass through a sieve into a clean pan. Re-heat and season to taste.

Lentil and Landcress Soup

Rainbow's End, Glastonbury
Chef; Shelagh Spear

1 tablespoon vegetable oil
1 onion, peeled and chopped
5 oz (150g) red lentils
2 pints (generous litre) water
generous bunch of landcress (or two of watercress)
2 tablespoons shoyu
lemon juice
black pepper

Landcress is a very useful addition to the kitchen garden. It looks like watercress but thrives without water. It is more pungent and aromatic than watercress but for this recipe watercress can be substituted if you cannot track down landcress.

Pour the oil into your soup pan. Add to it the onion and sweat it for a moment or two with the lid on.

Add the lentils and water. Bring to the boil, skim off any scum and simmer until the lentils are soft and "mushy".

Meanwhile prepare your cress: trim off any stringy stems and discoloured leaves. Wash thoroughly.

Add the washed cress to the boiling liquid and cook briefly, for say 3 minutes.

Take the soup off the heat and purée it in a liquidiser or food processor.

Finally, add the shoyu sauce and season to taste with lemon juice and black pepper. Reheat to serve. (I like to give the soup a final gloss with a knob of butter, but of course a milk free vegetable margarine can be used for vegans, or it can be left out altogether.)

Mushrooms Marinière

Food for Friends, Brighton
Chef; Simon Hope

1 lh (450g) whole button mushrooms, washed and trimmed
3 oz (75g) shallots, peeled and finely chopped
1 oz (25g) parsley stalks
1 oz (25g) butter or vegetable margarine
1 pint (575ml) dry white wine
1 pint (575ml) vegetable stock
4 oz (125g) butter or vegetable margarine
2 oz (50g) wholewheat flour
2 dessertspoons cream
1 oz (25g) parsley, chopped
juice of 1 lemon
4 cloves garlic, crushed
1 sheet of nori seaweed, toasted and crumbled

A soup which could be a main course if served with large chunks of hot wholewheat garlic bread.

Sauté the mushrooms, shallots and parsley stalks in a little butter.

Add the wine and reduce by a third.

Add the stock and bring to the boil. Beat the butter and flour together to form a beurre manié. Whisk this into the soup as it boils gently.

Finish the soup by adding the cream, chopped parsley, lemon juice and garlic. Sprinkle over the nori.

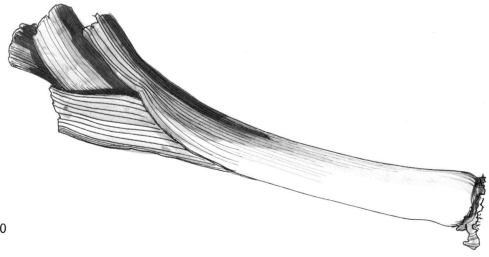

Curried Parsnip Soup

Herbs, Coventry
Chef; Robert Jackson

4 tablespoons vegetable oil
1 teaspoon curry powder
4 sticks celery
1 medium carrot
2 medium onions
1 ½ lb (700g) parsnips
1 vegetable stock cube
1 ½ pints (900ml) water
6 fl oz (175ml) milk
4 fl oz (125ml) single cream
salt and black pepper

Put the oil in a large saucepan, stir in the curry powder and cook for two minutes to develop the flavour.

Roughly chop the vegetables, then add them to the oil and cook gently for 5 minutes.

Add the water and stock cube. Bring to the boil, cover and simmer for 25–30 minutes.

Either liquidise the soup or pass through a sieve into a clean saucepan.

Add the milk and cream and season to taste. Reheat gently and adjust the consistency if necessary (cornflour to thicken or milk to thin).

Garnish with a thin slice of apple dipped in lemon juice and chopped parsley.

For a low calorie version, substitute the cream for yoghurt and use skimmed milk.

Pimento Soup with White Wine and Cheese   *Serves 4–6*

Food For Thought, London
Chef; Kit Norman

1 medium onion, chopped
a little oil
2 sticks celery, chopped
4 red peppers, seeded and chopped
1 green pepper, seeded and chopped
1 cup dry white wine
2 cups vegetable stock or hot water
¼ teaspoon whole cumin seeds
a pinch of basil and marjoram
salt and pepper
4 oz (125g) very mature cheddar cheese, grated
fresh chives for garnish, chopped

Fry the onion in a little oil for a few minutes, then add the celery and peppers and cook until soft.

Add the wine and simmer for a further 5 minutes.

Add the stock, cumin seeds and season sparingly with herbs, salt and pepper.

Remove from the heat, liquidize. Return to the heat until just below boiling point.

Gradually stir in the grated cheese until completely melted.

Check the seasoning and garnish with plenty of chopped chives.

NOTE If you do not have a blender, simply chop the vegetables finely and neatly before cooking.

Potato and Fennel Soup

Serves 6

Lakeland Hedgerow, Bowness on Windermere
Chefs; Jennifer Mason and Stephen Davy

1 onion, chopped
oil
2 large potatoes, peeled and chopped
2 heads fennel, washed and chopped
1 pint (575ml) vegetable stock
1 pint (575ml) milk
salt and pepper
nutmeg
double cream
chopped parsley

Sauté the onion in a little oil until soft. Add the potatoes and fennel and cook for two minutes.

Add the vegetable stock and simmer until the potatoes are tender.

Leave to cool slightly then put through a blender until smooth.

Return the soup to a pan, add the milk and reheat to serving temperature. Season to taste with salt, pepper and nutmeg.

Serve with a dash of cream and a sprinkling of chopped parsley.

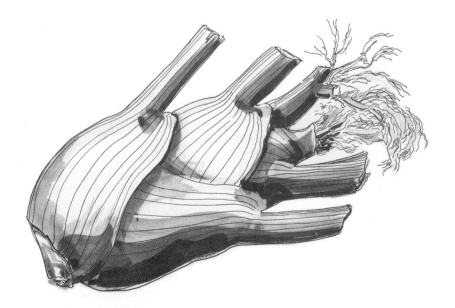

Spinach Soup

Serves 6

Nuthouse, London
Chef; Abraham Nasr

4 oz (125g) onion, chopped
2 oz (50g) margarine
4 oz (125g) potato, diced
8 oz (225g) fresh spinach
1 teaspoon mixed spice
½ teaspoon ground cumin
lemon juice (optional)

Lightly fry the onion in the margarine until light brown. Add the potato and 2 cups of water and bring to the boil. Cook for 5 minutes. Test the potato and cook longer if necessary.

Chop the spinach and add to the potato mixture with the spice and cumin. Return to the boil for a couple of minutes.

Liquidise the soup. Return to a clean saucepan, re-heat and add lemon juice if desired.

Cream of Watercress Soup

Serves 4

Good Earth, Wells
Chef; Tina Dearling

1 oz (25g) butter
1 onion, chopped
1 medium potato, peeled and chopped
2 bunches watercress, shredded
¾ pint (400ml) milk
½ pint (275ml) vegetable stock
salt and pepper
4 tablespoons cream

Gently fry the onion, potato and watercress in the butter for 5 minutes.

Add the milk and stock, cover, and cook for a further 15 minutes. Remove from the heat and liquidise.

44

Return the soup to the heat and season to taste, and finally stir in the cream.

Serve with wholemeal bread.

Black Eyed Bean Terrine

Serves 6–8

Huckleberry's, Bath
Chef; Kaye Bromley

1 medium onion, chopped
8 cloves garlic, crushed
1 ½ teaspoons cumin
1 tablespoon chopped parsley
1 medium cooking apple
12 oz (350g) black eyed beans, soaked overnight and cooked
1 tablespoon tamari
1 tablespoon tahini
salt and pepper
5 large carrots, diced
1 oz (25g) butter
salt and pepper
oil for frying
fresh herbs to garnish

Sauté the onion, garlic, cumin and parsley. When almost cooked, add the apple and cover the pan, cooking until the apple is soft.

Blend the mixture with the black eyed beans, tamari, tahini, and salt and pepper until very smooth.

Boil the carrots in a little water until soft. Drain and blend with the butter until soft.

Line a large loaf tin (7" × 4", 18cm × 10cm) with greaseproof paper. Place the bean mixture and the carrot mixture into the tin in alternate layers (starting with the bean mixture).

Cook at 300°F/150°C/Gas 2 for about 2 hours.

Remove from the oven, leave to cool and turn out on to a flat dish. Garnish with fresh herbs.

Cashew Nut Pâté

York Wholefood, York
Chef; Brid Coady Weekes

4 oz (125g) cashews, roasted and finely ground
11 oz (300g) cottage cheese
2–3 fl oz (50–75ml) single cream
juice of ½ lemon (or to taste)
1 clove of garlic, crushed
2–3 tablespoons chopped parsley
½–1 tablespoons chopped garden herbs (e.g. marjoram, thyme, basil and
  perhaps a little rosemary)

Roast the cashew nuts on a baking tray in the oven at 300°F/150°C/Gas Mark 2 for 10–15 minutes until lightly and evenly browned.

Grind the nuts in a coffee mill (clean it by grinding a crust of bread and wiping out with a soft, dry cloth), a hand mill or a mouli.

Blend the cottage cheese, cream and juice in a blender, or through a mouli or sieve, until it is smooth.

Beat in the cashews, garlic and herbs and chill.

Serve with crackers or oatcakes and raw garnish.

Mint Pâté

That Café, Machester
Chef; Joseph Quinn

1 lb (450g) black-eyed beans, soaked overnight in cold water
1 large onion, diced
3 cloves garlic, peeled
1 small jar of mint sauce
olive oil to taste

Drain the beans, place in a saucepan and cover with fresh water to a level 3" (8 cm) above the beans. Bring to the boil and simmer for about 1 hour, until the beans are soft. Drain.

Sauté the onion and garlic in olive oil until the onions are translucent. Mix together with the beans and mint sauce and mash until you achieve a texture you like. Add more oil to taste.

Pile into a serving dish or into ramekins and serve with toast or pitta bread and a side salad.

Mushroom and Celery Pâté

Serves 4–6

Gannets, Newark
Chef; Hilary Bower

3 oz (75g) butter
1 medium onion, finely chopped
2 cloves garlic, crushed
3 sticks celery, chopped
8 oz (225g) mushrooms, sliced
1 tablespoon lemon juice
grated rind ½ a lemon
1 level tablespoon chopped parsley
salt and pepper
2 level teaspoons mixed herbs
2 level tablespoons flour
3 fl oz (75ml) double cream
clarified butter
lemon twists
sprigs of parsley

Melt the butter in a large frying pan. Add the finely chopped onion and cook over a medium flame until slightly softened. Add the crushed garlic, cook for another 1 or 2 minutes and then add the sliced mushrooms, lemon juice and rind, parsley, seasoning and mixed herbs.

Stir in the flour and continue to cook for a few more minutes. Add the double cream, turn up the heat and reduce the mixture.

The mixture is now ready to be puréed (or Magimixed). Mix until smooth and even in texture.

Put into a suitable pâté pot and allow to cool. Top with a little clarified butter and decorate with lemon twists and a sprig of parsley.

Mushroom Hazelnut and Red Wine Pâté

Serves 4–6

Wild Oats II, Bristol
Chef; Nicky Smith

1 large Spanish onion, coarsely chopped
8 oz (225g) flat open mushrooms, coarsely chopped
3 teaspoons cayenne pepper
3 tablespoons unrefined sunflower oil
1 tablespoon shoyu
1 fl oz (25ml) red wine
1 clove garlic, crushed
fresh ginger to taste (optional)
1 teaspoon rosemary
1 teaspoon thyme
2 oz (50g) wholewheat breadcrumbs
2 oz (50g) hazelnuts, dry roasted and chopped
2 oz (50g) peanuts, dry roasted and chopped

Sauté together the onion, mushrooms and cayenne pepper in the oil until the mushrooms start to release their juices.

Add the shoyu and red wine. Add the garlic, ginger (if being used), and herbs and cover the pan. Leave to cook for a few minutes. Cook the vegetables at boiling point for 3 minutes then add the breadcrumbs and nuts.

Put the mixture in a food processor and process just enough to combine the ingredients without making the mixture too smooth. It should have a coarse texture and be wet enough to just "slump". Taste, and add more wine, herbs, cayenne or shoyu as you prefer.

Place the mixture in a small bread tin and bake at 475°F/180°C/Gas 5 for an hour on the middle shelf.

When the pâté is cooked it will still appear to be fairly "slumpy" and only thickens up as it cools. When it is completely cold turn the pâté out on to a rectangular dish and garnish. Serve in slices with wholemeal bread or toast and garlic butter.

Spicy Peanut Dip with Crudités

Serves 4

Quarry Shop, Machynlleth
Chef; Anne Lowmass

8 oz (225g) peanuts
3 cloves garlic, crushed
1 tablespoon tomato purée
2 tablespoons sunflower oil
1 tablespoon chopped parsley
1 teaspoon ground cumin
1 teaspoon ground coriander
1 small red chilli or 1 teaspoon chilli powder
2 tablespoons peanut butter
tomato juice or water

For the crudités:

Choose a selection of fresh vegetables; carrots, cucumbers, courgettes,
peppers, celery, fennel, radishes, mouli, cauliflower, spring onions, lettuce,
chicory, firm avocados are all excellent

Roast the peanuts on a tray in the oven until they are brown, then grind them finely in
a liquidiser or pestle and mortar.

Add the other ingredients except the tomato juice or water and mix well. Gradually add
the liquid (through the hole in the lid of the liquidiser, if using one) until the dip is
smooth and creamy. If you are making it by hand add the liquid a little at a time,
beating well between each addition.

Pile the dip into a bowl and arrange the raw vegetables, cut into long thin strips or
finger sized pieces, around it. It is good served with warm pitta bread too.

Tofu, Cashew and Carrot Dip

Delany's, Shrewsbury

8 oz (225g) cashew nuts
2 oz (50g) wholemeal breadcrumbs
1 carton (11 oz/300g) tofu
8 oz (225g) finely grated carrot
2 oranges
2 cloves garlic, crushed
salt and black pepper
1 bunch spring onions, chopped

Delicious used as a dip or spread, on bread or biscuits, or served with a selection of fresh vegetables.

Finely chop the cashew nuts (preferably in a food processor). Add to them the breadcrumbs, tofu and carrot. Mix to a smooth paste.

Finely grate the rind from both oranges and squeeze the juice from one. Add the rind and juice to the cashew mixture with the garlic and salt and pepper. Mix to a smooth consistency.

Serve garnished with chopped spring onion.

Watercress Dip

Marno's, Ipswich
Chef; Marianne

1 large bunch watercress
1 teaspoon green peppercorns (optional)
5 fl oz (150ml) yoghurt
4 oz (125g) cream cheese
4 oz (125g) low fat cheese (curd or Quark)
raw vegetables, to garnish

Pick over the watercress, removing larger stalks and any yellow leaves. Wash thoroughly and dry well. Place in a blender or food processor with the peppercorns, if used, and the yoghurt. Blend until smooth and green.

Put the cheese in a mixing bowl, mash with a fork and gradually add the watercress mixture.

To serve, divide the mixture between 4 individual bowls. Serve accompanied by a selection of raw vegetables suitable for dipping, e.g. cucumber sections, slices of carrot and pepper, cauliflower florets. A few coarsely chopped walnuts sprinkled over the top makes a nice crunchy addition.

Asparagus with Eggs Mollet

Serves 4

Everyman Bistro, Liverpool

1–2 lb (450–900g) asparagus (the amount depends on your purse)
4 eggs, free range if possible
sea salt to taste

Asparagus is one of the delights of the year, and although it may be expensive, you won't have to have fillet steak to accompany it. Nor does it have to be just a starter to a multi-coarse meal. Accompany this recipe with minted new potatoes or some good wholemeal bread and a plain green salad of crisp chilled cos lettuce leaves. This is a feast that won't cost you a fortune.

Prepare the asparagus. Using a small knife, peel away the tough skin from each stalk. If you start at the base of the stem and work towards the tips you should find that the most is cut away at the start, tapering away to nothing as you approach the tips. Tie the stalks into equal sized bundles, using up to a 1 lb (450g) in each bundle.

Heat up a large pan of salted water. It should be large enough for the asparagus to be laid lengthways in the water without being crushed up against the sides and for all the bundles to be fully immersed throughout the cooking time.

Once the water has come to the boil carefully lower in the bundles of asparagus. Bring the water back to the boil and simmer for 5–10 minutes. The cooking time will depend upon the thickness of the asparagus and the size of the bundles, but it will be ready when the stalks are still slightly firm and the tips are only slightly limp.

Five to six minutes before you think the asparagus will be cooked gently lower the eggs into medium boiling water. Eggs mollet are halfway between soft-boiled and hard-boiled. Now gather your friends/family around your dining table and serve the asparagus on one large plate immediately it is cooked. Place the eggs alongside the spears. Don't bother to shell the eggs, but just cut off the tops. Now the diners dip the asparagus into the eggs and then season with salt as required.

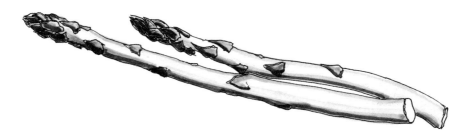

Hot Stuffed Avocados

Clinch's Salad House, Chichester
Chef; Alison Ellis

4oz (125g) mixed nuts, roughly chopped
2oz (50g) fresh wholemeal breadcrumbs
1–2 tablespoons mixed fresh herbs, parsley, marjoram and chives, chopped
    finely
4 oz (125g) cheddar cheese, grated
6 ripe tomatoes, skinned and chopped finely
tomato purée to taste
1 small clove garlic, finely chopped
small piece fresh ginger, peeled and finely chopped
tabasco to taste
4–6 tablespoons dry sherry
3 large avocado pears
lemon juice
2oz (50g) Cheddar cheese, grated

Mix together in a large bowl the nuts, breadcrumbs, herbs, cheese, tomatoes, tomato purée, garlic, ginger and tabasco. Finally add enough sherry to give the mixture a pâté like consistency. This forms the stuffing for the avocados and can be made in advance.

Just before you want to cook the dish, skin and stone the pears and brush them all over with lemon juice to prevent them discolouring.

Pile a sixth of the stuffing mixture onto each pear half and roughly shape into a dome. Place in a shallow baking dish and sprinkle with the remaining cheese. Bake at once at 400°F/200°C/Gas 6 for about 20 minutes until hot and bubbly.

Broccoli and Chestnut Gougère

Food For Friends, Brighton
Chef; Tracy West

Serves 4

¼ pint (150ml) water or milk, or a mixture of the two
2 oz (50g) butter
1 teaspoon salt
3 oz (75g) wholewheat flour, sifted and then add the bran back
3 free-range eggs
3 oz (75g) grated Gruyère cheese

For the filling:

1 oz (25g) butter or vegetable margarine
1 lb (450g) broccoli, cut into spears
1 large green pepper, diced
4 oz (125g) cooked chestnuts
1 teaspoon ginger
sherry glass of dry Martini
1 tablespoon shoyu
1 pint (575ml) sour cream
salt and pepper
garlic, to taste (optional)
1 bunch chives

An attractive dish, guaranteed to set a dinner party alight. The gougère, or choux ring, may be prepared in advance, but must at least be warm when the filling is added. If you have allowed the ring to cool down completely, place it on a baking tray in a low oven, with some foil covering the top, for about half an hour. This should give it time to heat through without overcooking. The chestnuts in the recipe will probably be dried and so will need soaking overnight and then cooking. Fresh chestnuts can be used but they do tend to be hairy. Water chestnuts work very well.

Place the water, butter and salt in a large, heavy saucepan. Melt the butter and bring the water to the boil, then remove from the heat and stir in the flour. Continue to cook, stirring all the time until the mixture leaves the side of the pan. Remove it from the heat and allow to cool slightly. Beat in the eggs one at a time and then the cheese.

Fit a piping bag with a 1–2″ (2.5–5cm) nozzle and fill the bag with the paste. On a greased baking sheet pipe either one large ring or four equal sized rings. Bake at 400°F/200°C/Gas 6 for 30 minutes until the ring(s) is well risen and slightly crisp.

Make the filling. Heat the fat in a deep pan. Sauté the broccoli and green pepper for 5 minutes. Add the chestnuts and ginger and continue cooking for a further 5 minutes.

When everything is very hot add the dry Martini, reduce by half over a high heat and add the shoyu, sour cream and seasoning. If you like, add a little garlic too.

Pour the sauce into the centre of the gougère, taking care not to spill it over the sides. Serve immediately sprinkled with chopped chives.

Cheese and Millet Croquettes au Gratin
Serves 6

Herbs, Coventry
Chef; Robert Jackson

1 ½ pints (900ml) water
½ teaspoon mixed herbs
½ teaspoon basil
1 pinch of cayenne pepper
10 oz (275g) millet
1 small red or green pepper
1 medium onion
3 tablespoons oil
1 clove garlic, crushed
2 oz (50g) frozen sweetcorn niblets
8 oz (225g) Cheddar, grated
1 tablespoon chopped parsley
salt and black pepper

For the coating:

flour
beaten egg
wholemeal breadcrumbs

For the sauce:

3 oz (75g) butter
3 heaped tablespoons flour
1 ½ pints (900ml) milk
2 oz (50g) grated cheddar
salt and black pepper
2 oz (50g) Cheddar, grated
1 oz (25g) Parmesan

Bring water and herbs to the boil in a large saucepan, stir in millet and simmer gently for approximately 25 minutes, stirring frequently, until all the water is absorbed.

Seed the pepper and dice finely. Chop the onion finely. Heat the oil and sauté the vegetables with the crushed garlic until soft.

Cook the sweetcorn in boiling water for approximately 3 minutes. Drain the water off.

Add all the cooked vegetables, cheese and parsley to the millet. Season well and mix to combine everything thoroughly. Leave to get cold.

Mould the mix into approximately 12 croquettes, shaping them neatly by hand.

Dip each croquette first into the flour, then beaten egg and finally the wholemeal breadcrumbs.

Fry in either deep or shallow oil until crisp and golden brown all over. Put on to absorbent paper and keep warm.

Prepare the sauce. Melt the butter and add the flour. Mix well and cook for 1 minute. Slowly add the milk, stirring all the time to avoid lumps. If lumps should form, don't worry, a few beats with a balloon whisk will solve the problem. When all the milk has been added, carefully bring the sauce to the boil, stirring all the time. Simmer gently for 3 minutes. Add the grated cheese and beat until smooth. Season with salt and pepper.

Lay the croquettes in a warm gratin dish. Carefully spoon the sauce over the croquettes and sprinkle lightly with grated cheddar and Parmesan. Put under a hot grill and leave until brown. Sprinkle with chopped fresh parsley and serve.

Apple, Stilton and Walnut Flan
Serves 6

Clinchs Salad House, Chichester
Chef; Alison Ellis

For the pastry:

6 oz (175g) plain wholemeal flour
1 level teaspoon baking powder
pinch of salt
1 ½ oz (40g) margarine
1 ½ oz (40g) vegetable fat
approx 2 tablespoons cold water

For the filling:

2 firm eating apples (Cox's are nice)
4 oz (125g) Stilton cheese

3 oz (75g) walnuts
2 eggs, beaten
5 fl oz (150ml) milk or cream
chives, finely chopped
salt and pepper

Make the pastry. Sieve the flour, baking powder and salt together and then rub in the margarine. Gradually add enough water to make a firm dough.

Roll out the pastry and line an 8″ (20cm) flan tin, prick the base and leave to one side to rest for at least 30 minutes. Bake blind at 400°F/200°C/Gas Mark 6 until the pastry is lightly browned. While the pastry is cooking make the filling.

Wash the apples, but do not peel them, then dice them finely. Crumble the Stilton and roughly chop the walnuts and then mix them all together with the beaten eggs, cream or milk, chives and seasoning.

Pour the filling into the flan case and bake for 40–50 minutes until the mixture has set and is lightly browned.

Cottage Cheese and Watercress Flan

Serves 6

Nature's Way, Eastbourne
Chef; Dorothy and Maurice Fossitt

1 × 7″ (18cm) cooked wholemeal savoury flan case
12 oz (350g) cottage cheese
2 oz (50g) chopped pineapple (fresh or tinned)
2 oz (50g) chopped cucumber
1 oz (25g) chopped mushrooms
2 tomatoes, seeded and chopped
2 sticks celery, chopped
1 bunch watercress, chopped (keep a few sprigs for decoration)
black pepper to taste

Mix all the filling ingredients together until evenly distributed. Taste for seasoning.

Pile the filling firmly into the flan case and decorate with sprigs of watercress.

Serve chilled.

This filling can be used equally successfully in individual flan cases.

Cottage Cheese Cooler

Neal's Yard Bakery, London
Chef; Rachel Haigh

1 lb (450g) cottage cheese
1 stalk celery
½ cucumber
1 small red pepper
1 medium sized carrot
1 tablespoon parsley
1 lemon
1 teaspoon sesame seeds

Put the cottage cheese into a mixing bowl.

Chop the celery, cucumber and red pepper into small pieces. Add to the cottage cheese.

Grate the carrot and chop the parsley finely. Add to the cottage cheese mix.

Grate and juice the lemon and pour over the cottage cheese.

Mix everything together gently and turn into individual dishes. Sprinkle with sesame seeds and serve with hot corn muffins.

Eggs à la . . .

Serves 4–6

Cnapan, Newport
Chef; Eluned Lloyd

1 large onion, finely chopped
1 clove garlic, crushed
2 tablespoons oil
6 fresh tomatoes
1 small tin tomatoes
1 teaspoon coriander
1 teaspoon cumin
1 pinch chilli powder
1 dessertspoon wine vinegar
brown sugar to taste
2 oz (50g) sultanas
salt and black pepper
6 hard boiled eggs

For the topping:

4–6 oz (125–175g) wholemeal breadcrumbs
oil for frying
a pinch of basil

sprinkling of Parmesan cheese
fresh limes to garnish

A starter based on eggs served with a sauce that can be altered to suit the ingredients you have available.

Sauté the onion and garlic in the oil.

Skin the fresh tomatoes and chop. Add to the pan with the tinned tomatoes, herbs, spices, vinegar, sugar and sultanas. Simmer gently for 20 minutes with the lid on until the flavours are infused. Taste for seasoning.

Make the topping. Fry the crumbs in the oil until they are really crunchy. Do not leave them when they are cooking because they catch easily. Drain well on kitchen paper, then toss in a pinch of basil.

Cut the eggs in half, and lay cut side down in a flat dish. Pour over the "à la" sauce and cover with the crunchy crumbs. Sprinkle over the Parmesan cheese and flash under a very hot grill. Garnish with fresh limes and serve immediately.

59

Gnocchi alla Phillipo

Food For Friends, Brighton
Chef; Phil Taylor

1 pint (575ml) milk
6 oz (175g) brown rice semolina
½ teaspoon nutmeg
salt and pepper
1 egg yolk
2 oz (50g) Parmesan cheese
2 oz (50g) butter

For the tomato sauce:

1 tablespoon olive oil
1 medium onion, finely chopped
2 oz (50g) carrots, finely chopped
1 oz (25g) celery, finely chopped
½ bayleaf
2 teaspoons fresh thyme
2 cloves garlic, crushed
1 oz (25g) wholewheat flour
2 tablespoons tomato purée
1 pint (575ml) vegetable stock or ½ pint (275ml) stock and ½ pint (275ml)
   red wine
1 teaspoon honey
salt and pepper
soya sauce

This dish is a delicious starter and may be cooked in two stages, preferably the day before it is due to be eaten. Both the gnocchi and the sauce are nicest if allowed to "settle" in a fridge for 12 hours.

Make the gnocchi. Bring the milk to the boil, add the semolina and whisk well to avoid lumps. Season with nutmeg, salt and pepper. Cook gently for 8 minutes, stirring continuously. Remove from the heat, beat in the egg yolk and half the Parmesan. Pour into a shallow tray (preferably stainless steel) that has previously been buttered. Smooth out until the mixture is ½" (1cm) thick all over. Spread half the butter over the surface (you may find it easier to melt it first). Allow to chill for as long as possible.

Using a 2" (5cm) round cutter cut out circles of gnocchi. Place the remnants in the bottom of an ovenproof dish and arrange the circles neatly over the top. Sprinkle over the remaining Parmesan and melted butter. Place in the oven at 400°F/200°C/Gas 6 until the tops are nicely browned.

Make the sauce. Sauté the vegetables and herbs in the oil until the vegetables are beginning to soften. Add the garlic and the flour, cook for a minute, then add the tomato purée and the stock. Return to the boil, mix in the honey and simmer for an hour or so until the sauce has thickened sufficiently – it should coat the back of a wooden spoon. Stir frequently to avoid sticking. Season with salt, pepper and soya sauce.

To serve pour the sauce around the gnocchi in a ribbon.

Guacamole

Serves 6

Food For Health, London
Chef; Lorraine Mansoir Rahman

2 large tomatoes
1 clove garlic and/or ½ small onion
1–2 fresh green chilli peppers seeded or ¼ teaspoon cayenne pepper
juice of ½ lemon, plus more to taste
good pinch salt and freshly ground black pepper
2 ripe avocado pears

Skin the tomatoes, cut them into quarters and take out the centre and seeds. Place the tomatoes in a food processor or blender and add the crushed garlic, chopped onion, peppers, lemon juice, and seasoning.

Cut the pears in half and remove the stone. With a large teaspoon, scoop all the flesh into the blender. Blend together until smooth – but you can still see flecks of red in the mixture. Taste and adjust the seasoning.

Serve in small bowls as a dip with raw vegetables or with some freshly baked wholemeal rolls. Sprinkle the top with a little chopped parsley or coriander. Use the guacamole immediately if possible, if not, store under cling film in the fridge and give a good stir before serving.

Cheesy Leek Tarts

Wholemeal Café, London
Chef; Liz Austin

For the pastry:

3 tablespoons oil
salt to taste
6 tablespoons hot water
6 oz (175g) wholemeal flour

For the filling:

2 medium leeks
2 oz (50g) butter
1 teaspoon basil
5 oz (150g) cream cheese
5 oz (150g) sour cream
1 teaspoon shoyu
1 teaspoon made mustard
salt and pepper to taste
2 oz (50g) Cheddar cheese, grated
sesame seeds

Make the pastry. Mix the oil, salt and water together. Gradually add the flour until a pliable dough if formed. You may need a little more than the 6 oz (175g). Allow to cool. Roll out and cut into circles to form tarts (you should be able to make about 12). Bake at 375°F/190°C/Gas 5 for 15 minutes, or until just brown.

Make the filling. Finely chop the leeks and fry in the butter with the basil until soft. Stir in the flour to make a roux. Remove from the heat, add the cream cheese, sour cream, shoyu, mustard and salt and pepper to taste. It should be a very thick mixture. Cool for about 30 minutes then spoon generously into the pastry cases.

Sprinkle the grated Cheddar and sesame seeds over the top of each tart and cook at 400°F/200°C/Gas 6 for about 10 minutes until the cheese is golden brown. Serve immediately with a garnish of watercress and tomato.

Leek and Blue Cheese Soufflé

Serves 6

Cranks, London

6 oz (175g) leeks, trimmed and thinly sliced
1 oz (25g) butter or margarine
ground nutmeg to taste
salt and pepper to taste
2 oz (50g) soft textured blue cheese, crumbled
½ oz (15g) 100% wholemeal flour
5 fl oz (150ml) milk
2 oz (50g) Cheddar cheese, grated
pinch cayenne
¼ teaspoon sage
2 tablespoons parsley, chopped
2 eggs, separated

This is an impressive starter – make sure your guests are "at the ready"! The leek mixture and the sauce can be made in advance. Reheat gently, but do not add the egg whites until the last minute. For a main course double the quantities and serve in larger dishes.

Wash the leeks and drain them well. Melt half the butter in a pan, add the leeks and cook until just tender. Remove from the heat and season with nutmeg, salt and pepper. Stir in the blue cheese and mix well. Divide the mixture evenly between 6 buttered ramekins.

Melt the remaining butter in a pan, stir in the flour and cook for a few seconds then stir in the milk. Continue to stir over the heat until the sauce boils and thickens. Remove from the heat, add the Cheddar cheese, cayenne and sage and season well with salt and pepper. Cool slightly, then add the chopped parsley and egg yolks. Mix thoroughly. Beat the egg whites until stiff peaks form. Using a metal spoon, carefully fold approximately 1 tablespoon of the egg white into the cheese sauce, then fold in the remainder.

Spoon the soufflé mixture over the leeks and bake in the oven at 375°F/190°C/Gas 5 for about 20 minutes or until risen and golden. Serve immediately.

Reproduced from *Entertaining With Cranks,* by Kay Canter and Daphne Swann. Published by JM Dent & Sons Ltd.

Masala Dhosa

Sree Krishna, London
Chef; Mr Ramanarayan

For the Dhosa:

1 lb (450g) ground rice flour
5 oz (150g) urad dall flour
water
salt
oil

This is a southern Indian version of a crispy pancake stuffed with a spicy potato filling.

Mix the ground rice flour and the urad dall flour with enough water to make a pancake style mixture. Leave this mixture overnight then when ready to cook add salt to taste and, if necessary, more water until the batter is runny.

Heat a griddle or large frying pan with a scant amount of oil, when it is very hot pour a circle of the mixture on and after a few moments dribble some oil on top of the pancake. There is no need to turn it, when it is browned all over remove from the pan and start the next one; the mixture should make about 10 dhosas.

The prepared masala should be spooned on one side and the dhosa folded over. Serve immediately.

For the Masala:

8 oz (225g) urad dall (black gram)
2 lb (900g) potatoes
1 dessertspoon black mustard seeds
1½ in (4cm) fresh ginger, chopped
2 onions, sliced lengthwise
2 green chillis, chopped
1 teaspoon turmeric
salt

These are best served with a cool coconut chutney or a bowl of yoghurt and chopped cucumber.

Boil the potatoes without salt and mash them.

Cook the urad dall with water until soft.

Heat oil in a frying pan and add the mustard seeds, chillis, ginger, onions, dall, turmeric and salt. Cook this mixture until all the ingredients are soft, then spoon in the potatoes and mix well.

Mushrooms in Garlic and Cider

Serves 4

Saxon's, Brighton
Chef; Saxon Howard

4 cloves garlic
4 fl oz (150ml) olive oil
pinch of cayenne pepper
salt
½ onion, very finely sliced
1 lb (450g) mushrooms, washed and trimmed
1 teaspoon mustard powder
1 teaspoon oregano
½ pint (275ml) dry cider
1 dessertspoon tamari or bouillon
plenty of black pepper
bread to serve

Crush the garlic and put in a pan with the oil, cayenne and a little salt. Cook over a medium heat until the garlic starts to brown.

Add the onion and cook for a further 2 minutes.

Add the mushrooms, and then the remaining ingredients and simmer for at least 5 minutes. If you can leave the mushrooms for another hour or two over a low heat the flavour intensifies splendidly.

Serve with plenty of bread to mop up the juices.

Mushrooms à la Grecque

Guild Café, Bristol

5 fl oz (150ml) olive oil
5 fl oz (150ml) water
juice of a large lemon
3 tomatoes, blanched, peeled and chopped very small
½ teaspoon thyme
1 bayleaf
salt and pepper
1 teaspoon coriander seeds, finely crushed
1 lb (450g) button mushrooms

Heat all the ingredients except the mushrooms in a large saucepan.

Clean the mushrooms and trim, but leave whole. When the liquid begins to boil add the mushrooms and cook for about ten minutes, stirring often so that the mushrooms can absorb as much juice as possible. Once tender, remove the mushrooms with a slotted spoon and put to one side.

Boil up the remaining liquid until it is thick, then return the mushrooms to it. The final result should not be swimming in juice, the sauce should be thick and cling to the mushrooms. This classic French dish is best served simply on a bed of crisp lettuce as a starter.

Mushroom Kiev

Quarry Shop, Machynlleth
Chef; Anne Lowmass

16 large cultivated button type mushrooms, with caps approximately 1½–2"
  (4–5cm) across
1 oz (25g) seasoned flour (approximately)
2 beaten eggs
4 oz (125g) fresh wholewheat breadcrumbs (approximately)
oil for deep frying
8 wooden cocktail sticks

For the garlic butter:

4 oz (125g) butter
2 cloves garlic, crushed
grated rind and juice of 1 small lemon
black pepper

Make the garlic butter. Cream the butter with the garlic, lemon rind and juice and freshly ground black pepper. Shape the butter into a rectangular block, wrap in foil and leave in the refrigerator until hard.

Wipe the mushrooms and twist out the stalks, removing them completely.

Cut the butter into 8 small pieces and sandwich each piece between two mushroom caps, filling the cavities left by the stalks. Fix the caps together with a cocktail stick.

Repeat for each pair of mushrooms.

Roll each pair lightly in the flour, then dip in the beaten egg and next roll in the breadcrumbs. Repeat this last process again to ensure that each is really well coated in egg and breadcrumbs.

Heat up the oil until it is hot enough to turn a small square of bread golden brown in about 30 seconds. Gently deep fry each pair of mushrooms for 3–5 minutes. You will probably be able to fry 4 pairs at a time, depending on the size of the pan. When they are cooked through they will rise to the top of the fat.

Drain and serve immediately garnished with a slice of lemon and a sprig of parsley.

Hot Mushrooms with Stilton

Serves 4

Dumb Waiter Bistro, Todmorden
Chef; Jeffrey Taylor

8 oz (225g) small button mushrooms
⅓ oz (15g) butter
¼ pint (150ml) milk
½ oz (15g) flour
seasoning
4 oz (125g) blue Stilton
4 fl oz (125ml) white wine
4 fl oz (135ml) cream

Wash the mushrooms and trim. Melt the butter in a pan, add the mushrooms and sweat for 1–2 minutes.

Melt ½ oz (15g) butter in a pan, stir in the flour and gradually add the milk. Stir until the sauce comes to the boil and thickens. Season.

Add the white sauce to the mushrooms, and then the crumbled Stilton. Cook for a further 2 minutes. Pour in the wine and simmer until the mushrooms are just tender. Finally stir in the cream and simmer for another couple of minutes.

Stuffed Mushrooms

Herbs, Coventry
Chef; Robert Jackson

2 cloves garlic
1 medium onion
4 oz (125g) walnuts
4 oz (125g) mushrooms (including stalks)
4 oz (125g) low fat soft cheese
2 eggs
½ teaspoon tarragon (optional)
⅛ teaspoon nutmeg
salt and black pepper
chopped parsley
4 large open mushrooms
2 tablespoons wholemeal breadcrumbs

Process onion and garlic to a light purée, or chop very finely.

Grind walnuts finely or crush inside a polythene bag using a rolling pin.

Process mushrooms to a light purée, or chop very finely.

Process together, cheese, eggs, tarragon and nutmeg, or cream the ingredients together in a large bowl.

Combine all the ingredients and process or beat well until smooth. Season to taste.

Wash mushroom caps and place on a lightly oiled baking dish or tin.

Pipe or spoon the stuffing into the mushrooms and sprinkle a few extra crumbs over the top.

Bake the mushrooms for approximately 10 minutes at 375°F/190°C/Gas 5.

These are particularly nice if served on a crisp wholemeal croûte, simply made by removing the crusts from a slice of brown bread, cutting it into four and frying quickly in a little oil until crisp. Place the mushrooms on top of the croûtons and sprinkle over a little chopped parsley.

Tamari Mushrooms

Serves 4

Richmond Harvest, Richmond
Head chef; Jenny Howell
Second chefs; Sandra Mahaney and Helene Shlamka

1 clove garlic, crushed
sprinkling of sesame seeds
1 tablespoon oil
1 lb (450g) whole button mushrooms
1–2 tablespoons tamari or soya sauce, to taste

Sauté the garlic and sesame seeds in a little oil.

Add the mushrooms and cook stirring well until they are quite tender.

Stir in the tamari or soya sauce to taste and bring to the boil. Serve immediately or allow to go cold and serve chilled.

✥ Main Dishes ✥

Aduki Casserole

Lakeland Hedgerow, Bowness on Windermere
Chefs; Jennifer Mason and Stephen Davy

oil
1 large onion, peeled and sliced
2 cloves garlic, finely chopped
2 sticks celery, chopped
6 carrots, peeled and chopped
½ Savoy cabbage, shredded
14 oz (400g) tin plum tomatoes, chopped
1 tablespoon tomato purée
salt and pepper
2 dessertspoons brown sugar
pinch ginger
1 lb (450g) cooked aduki beans
4 oz (125g) cashew nuts

Sauté the onion, garlic and celery in a little oil until the onion is transparent. Add the carrots and cook for 3 minutes.

Add the cabbage, tomatoes and tomato purée. Stir well. Season and add the sugar and ginger. Simmer for 10 minutes.

Finally stir in the cooked beans, cashew nuts and simmer for a further 5 minutes. Serve with a green salad and crusty wholemeal bread.

Armenian Casserole

Wild Oats II, Bristol
Chef; Sarah Wale

8 oz (225g) Hunza apricots, soaked for 2–3 hours and stoned
1 large onion, diced
1 large red pepper, sliced
5 medium sized carrots, grated
20 oz (575g) cooked seitan, cut into chunks
¾ teaspoon ground coriander
½ handful cumin seeds
8 oz (225g) tofu cream
sunflower oil
sea salt

Sauté the onion, pepper and carrot slowly in sunflower oil until tender. Stir in the coriander and cumin with a little sea salt. Leave on a low heat.

Fry the chunks of seitan in a wok of hot oil until they are all golden brown. Drain and add to the vegetables.

Stir in the tofu cream and finally the hunzas. Re-heat and serve.

Aubergine and Red Bean Bake

Serves 4

Marno's, Ispwich
Chef; Penny

1 medium aubergine
salt
1 large onion, chopped
oil for frying
1 clove garlic, crushed
1 tablespoon tomato purée
14 oz (400g) tin tomatoes, chopped
½ teaspoon mixed dried herbs
6 oz (175g) red kidney beans, soaked overnight and boiled (or 1 × 14 oz (400g)
    tin of kidney beans, drained and well rinsed)
6 oz (175g) grated cheese

Slice the aubergine into ¼" (½cm) slices, sprinkle them with salt and leave for 30 minutes. Rinse well, and squeeze out the excess moisture then pat them dry. This preparation removes any bitter juices from the aubergine and makes them less absorbent, so that the final dish is not too greasy.

While the aubergines are soaking, fry the onion in about a tablespoon of oil, adding the garlic when the onion is soft and golden. Stir in the tomato purée and then add the chopped, tinned tomatoes and the herbs. Stir well to mix. Bring to the boil and simmer very gently for 10 minutes.

Fry the prepared aubergine slices in relays until soft and lightly brown, using the minimum amount of fat to prevent sticking. A lid on the pan is often helpful. When all the aubergine is cooked you can start assembling the dish.

Put a layer of aubergine in the bottom of a casserole dish, followed by a layer of sauce, a layer of beans and then a sprinkling of cheese. Repeat until the casserole is full, but leave the beans out of the top layer so that the dish is topped with sauce and cheese.

Bake at 375°F/190°C/Gas 5 for about 30 minutes until heated through and bubbling round the edges and on top. This is delicious served with a green salad which complements the earthy flavours of the aubergine and beans.

Spiced Aubergines, Courgettes and Tomatoes   *Serves 6–8*

Guild Café, Bristol

2 aubergines, sliced finely
salt
1 dozen cardomoms, with husks removed
2 heaped teaspoons coriander seeds
2 heaped teaspoons cumin seeds
1 large onion, sliced
4 cloves garlic, crushed
3 tablespoons sunflower oil
1 lb (450g) courgettes, cut into ½" (1cm) rings
1 large tin (28 oz/800g) tomatoes, drain and chop, but keep the juice
1 tablespoon tomato purée
½ packed creamed coconut, dissolved in ½ pint (275ml) water
juice of 1 lemon
salt and pepper
chilli powder (optional)

Place the aubergine slices in a colander, sprinkling the layers with salt and cover with a weighted plate and leave for a couple of hours.

Grind the spices, or crush in a pestle and mortar. Take a large saucepan or flameproof casserole and heat the oil. Fry the spices for a few minutes, then add the onions and crushed garlic and cook until softened. Add the drained aubergines, the courgettes and turn frequently until all the oil is absorbed.

Add the tomatoes, tomato purée, coconut and lemon juice. Simmer gently, stirring occasionally until the vegetables are soft but not mushy. This will take about 25 minutes. If it should begin to dry up, add a little of the juice reserved from the tin of tomatoes.

Season to taste before serving, and if you prefer a fiercer dish, add a little chilli powder. Serve on a bed of rice with a garnish of hard boiled eggs, sweet mango chutney and a crisp green salad.

Black Eyed Beans in Brown Ale

Serves 4

Saxon's, Brighton
Chef; Saxon Howard

1 lb (450g) black eyed beans, soaked overnight
2 cloves garlic, crushed
4 tablespoons cooking oil
½ teaspoon cayenne
salt
2 onions, sliced
2 carrots, sliced
1 green pepper, sliced
8 oz (225g) mushrooms, sliced
1 teaspoon sage
1 teaspoon thyme
1 teaspoon mustard powder
½ pint (275ml) vegetable stock
½ pint (275ml) brown ale
miso to taste (about 4 tablespoons)
salt and pepper

Cook the beans in unsalted water until soft.

Sauté the garlic in the oil with the cayenne and salt. When golden add first the onions and then the rest of the vegetables in the order given. Cover the pan and cook for 10 minutes until the vegetables are slightly tender. Add the cooked beans.

Add the herbs, vegetable stock and brown ale. Bring to the boil then cover the pan and simmer for 20–30 minutes.

Taste and add miso, salt and pepper as required. Serve with brown rice or millet, plus green vegetables or a side salad.

Broccoli and Brie Crèpes

Serves 8

That Café, Manchester
Chef; Joseph Quinn

For the batter:

1 egg
3 oz (75g) white flour
1 oz (25g) wholemeal flour
½ pint (275ml) milk or soya milk
pinch of salt
black pepper to taste

For the filling:

2 lb (900g) broccoli, as fresh as possible
1 ½ lb (700g) brie cheese
olive oil, for cooking

Beat the egg and gradually add the milk to it while still beating. Add a pinch of salt. Mixing all the time, pour the egg and milk on to the flours and beat until completely mixed. Season with black pepper and leave to stand for about an hour, or longer if possible.

Steam the broccoli until cooked but still firm.

Cook the crèpes until golden brown and keep warm. This mixture should make 8–10 crèpes using a 6" (15cm) frying pan.

Fill the crèpes with the cooked broccoli and cut slices of cheese and place over the vegetable. Roll the crèpes, place on a baking tray, cover with tin foil and warm through in a low oven for about 5–10 minutes until the cheese has melted.

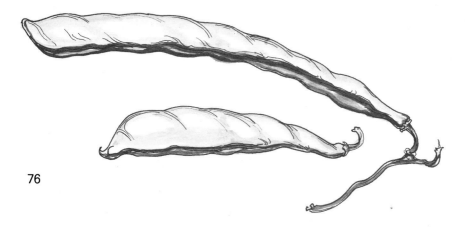

Bulghar Bake

Quarry Shop, Machynlleth
Chef; Anne Lowmass

a handful of sunflower seeds and sesame seeds
1 pint (575ml) bulghar wheat
oil
2 pints (generous litre) boiling water
salt and pepper
6 courgettes

For the sauce:

2 onions, finely chopped
1 red pepper, finely chopped
1 green pepper, finely chopped
2 cloves garlic, crushed
dried or fresh basil
flour
14 oz (400g) tin of tomatoes, liquidised or finely chopped
tamari
tahini
stock or water
small tin of sweetcorn, drained
fresh parsley, finely chopped
margarine

Fry the sunflower seeds, sesame seeds and bulghar in a large saucepan in oil for a few minutes, stirring often. Remove from the heat, add boiling water and cover. Leave for 15 minutes until the wheat has absorbed all the water and season.

Boil the courgettes in a pan of water for 10–15 minutes until they are just tender. Drain and set aside.

Fry the onions, pepper and garlic in a little oil with the basil. Add flour and stir to make a roux. Add the tomatoes, then the tahini, tamari and salt and pepper to taste. Add enough stock or water to make a thin sauce, and finally stir in the sweetcorn.

Take a large ovenproof dish and fill it with the following: a layer of bulghar, a layer of sliced courgettes, sauce, parsley, bulghar and then dot the top with margarine.

Bake for 20 minutes until brown on top.

Good Earth Cashew Nut Roast with Piquant Tomato Sauce

Good Earth, Wells
Chef; Tina Dearling

1 onion, chopped
2 oz (50g) butter
1 heaped teaspoon yeast extract
½ pint (275ml) water
12 oz (350g) ground cashewnuts
8 oz (225g) wholewheat breadcrumbs
1 teaspoon thyme or sage
1 teaspoon salt
black pepper
15 fl oz (425ml) tin of tomatoes, chopped

For the sauce:

2 oz (50g) butter
1 onion, chopped
1 clove garlic, crushed
1 oz (15g) 81% wholemeal flour
8 oz (225g) chopped tinned tomatoes
1 tablespoon tomato purée
½ pint (275ml) water or vegetable stock
1 teaspoon muscovado sugar
1 tablespoon cider vinegar
1 tablespoon Worcestershire sauce
½ teaspoon mixed herbs
salt and black pepper to taste
good pinch chilli powder

Make the roast. Fry the onion in the butter for 5 minutes. Dissolve the yeast extract in ½ pint (275ml) hot water. Mix all the ingredients together in a large basin. Grease a 2 pint (1 litre) baking dish, preferably earthenware. Place mixture into this and bake at 350°F/180°C/Gas 4 for about 30 minutes.

Make the sauce. Fry the onion and garlic in the butter until pale gold. Stir in the remaining ingredients. Bring to the boil, stirring continuously, then simmer gently for 25–30 minutes.

Check the sauce for seasoning. Serve portions of the nut roast coated with the sauce and accompanied by a crisp green salad or steamed vegetables.

Cauliflower and Courgette Lasagne

Serves 6–8

Hannah's, Worthing

1 large cauliflower, divided into florets
1 lb (450g) courgettes, sliced
1 ½ pints (900g) milk
4 oz (125g) margarine or butter
4 oz (125g) wholemeal flour
seasoning
8 oz (225g) mature Cheddar, grated
8 oz (225g) lasagne verdi, pre-cooked
4 hard boiled eggs
4 oz (125g) grated Cheddar

Lightly cook the cauliflower in boiling water for 3–4 minutes. Cook the courgettes in the same way.

Melt the butter in a large saucepan, stir in the flour and cook the roux for a couple of minutes. Gradually add the milk, then bring the sauce to the boil, stirring all the time. Season, stir in the grated cheese and remove from the heat.

Pour a thin layer of cheese sauce on the base of a large baking dish. Cover with a layer of lasagne, followed by the cauliflower, more lasagne and cheese sauce, the courgettes and finally a layer of lasagne and cheese sauce.

Finely chop in the boiled eggs. Mix in the grated cheese and spread over the top. Bake at 350°F/180°C/Gas 4 for about 35 minutes or until the top is golden brown.

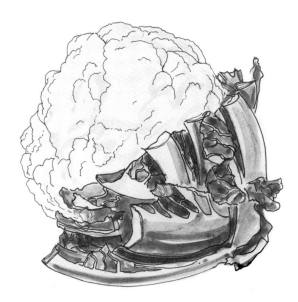

Celery, Apple and Cider Nut Roast

Wholemeal Vegetarian Café, London
Chef; Phil Downes

3 oz (75g) peanuts
3 oz (75g) hazelnuts
2 oz (50g) wholemeal breadcrumbs
1 medium onion, chopped
1 medium cooking apple, cored and chopped
2 sticks celery, chopped
2 tablespoons corn oil, for frying
1 teaspoon rosemary
1 teaspoon sage
2 tablespoons corn oil
1 tablespoon shoyu
2 tablespoons cider
1 egg, beaten
salt and pepper to taste
sunflower and sesame seeds for garnish

Roast the nuts in a medium hot oven until evenly browned and then grind or crush.

Fry the onion, apple and celery in a little oil with the rosemary and sage until soft. Add the nuts and breadcrumbs and then stir in the oil, shoyu, cider and beaten egg. Season.

Grease a small bread tin or roasting tin and fill with the nut mixture, pressing it down well. Sprinkle the seeds on top. Bake at 350°F/180°C/Gas 4 for 40 minutes. Serve with coleslaw and a green salad and some roast potatoes.

Celtic Pie

Serves 4

Cnapan, Newport
Chef; Eluned Lloyd

For the oaten crusty base:

4 oz (125g) margarine
2 tablespoons water
4 oz (125g) oats
3 oz (75g) wholemeal flour
salt

For the filling:

7 ½ oz (210g) tin of laverbread
2 fresh tomatoes
tarragon, or other herbs
1 onion, sliced into rings
olive oil for frying
4–6 oz (125–175g) tasty farmhouse cheese, sliced
1 orange juiced and zested
5 oz (150ml) natural yoghurt
2 eggs
4 tablespoons tinned sweetcorn
salt and black pepper
1 orange for garnish, peeled and sliced

Make the base. Melt the margarine, add the water and then the oats, flour and salt. Stir briskly. Line an 8½" (21cm) flan dish, using your fingers to press the oat mixture out.

Make the filling. Arrange a layer of fresh tomatoes on the base of the flan and sprinkle over a favourite herb (I use tarragon).

Fry the onion rings in a little olive oil and place on top of the tomatoes. Cover with the slices of cheese.

In a bowl, mix together the laverbread, orange juice and rind, yoghurt, eggs and sweetcorn. Pour this mixture over the cheese. Season.

Bake at 400°F/200°C/Gas 6 for 40–45 minutes until the mixture is set. Garnish with chunks of orange.

Courgette Fritters

Harvest Vegetarian, Ambleside
Chef; Gillian Kelly

6 medium sized courgettes, grated
6 oz (175g) grated Cheddar cheese
3 eggs
2 tablespoons chopped fresh parsley
2 teaspoons dried dill weed
2 teaspoons dried mint
salt and pepper
4 heaped tablespoons wheatmeal flour
oil, for frying

Mix together the grated courgette, cheese and eggs; then add the herbs and salt and pepper. Finally mix in the flour.

Shallow fry heaped dessertspoonfuls of the mixture until fairly firm and golden brown on both sides.

These are delicious hot or cold, and can be served with potatoes, rice and/or a crisp green salad. I particularly like to have them with a bowl of yoghurt (preferably sheep's) with garlic.

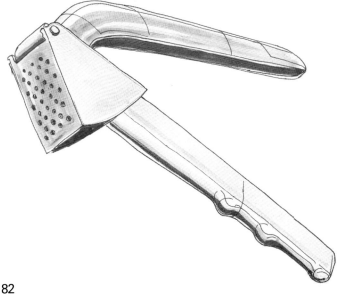

Kibbeh

Richmond Harvest, Richmond
Heaf chef; Jenny Howell
Second chefs; Sandra Mahaney and Helene Shlamka

1 small cauliflower, divided into small florets
8 oz (225g) millet
1½ pints (900ml) water
1 small onion, finely chopped
1 teaspoon cumin
salt to taste
1 large aubergine, diced and salted for 30 minutes and then drained
1 tablespoon oil
1 medium onion, finely sliced
2 cloves garlic, crushed
1 carrot, cut into strips
1 green pepper, finely sliced
6 oz (175g) mushrooms, sliced
2 teaspoons cinnamon
2 teaspoons coriander
5 fl oz (150ml) tamari or soya sauce
½ pint (275ml) water
salt and pepper
2 tablespoons sunflower seeds

Place the water, millet and cauliflower in a pan and simmer for about 20 minutes until all the water has been absorbed. Stir in the onion, cumin and salt to taste. Put to one side.

Sauté the onion and garlic in the oil until soft. Add the carrots and peppers and cook until they begin to soften. Stir in the mushrooms and aubergines. Stir well, cover and leave until the aubergines soften, stirring from time to time.

Stir in the spices and pour over the tamari and water. Bring to the boil and then simmer for a few minutes. Season. Pour into an ovenproof dish, top with the millet mixture and finally sprinkle over the sunflower seeds. Bake at 375°F/180°C/Gas 5 for 1 hour until brown.

Nuthouse Kofta

Nuthouse, London
Chef; Abraham Nasr

1 medium onion, finely chopped
4 oz (125g) vegetable margarine
2 oz (50g) mushrooms, finely chopped
2 oz (50g) potato, cooked and chopped finely
2 oz (50g) parsnip, cooked and chopped finely
8 oz (225g) swede, cooked and chopped finely
4 oz (125g) wheat, pre-soaked
8 oz (225g) medium oats
1½ teaspoons sage, or more to taste
salt and black pepper
2 fl oz (50ml) tomato juice
oil, for deep frying

It is important to chop the vegetables finely to ensure that the koftas don't fall apart when you are frying them. If you have a food processor it may be easier to process the vegetables together, after the addition of the tomato juice and egg until you have a semi-smooth consistency. The mixture is much easier to handle. It might also be easier to make a double quantity of the mixture and freeze half of it either just before the stage where you make the mixture into balls, or if you have the energy, complete all the balls except for frying, and freeze them like that.

Fry the onion in the margarine until soft. Add the mushrooms and cook for two or three minutes. Remove from the heat and add the pre-cooked vegetables, wheat, sage and seasoning. Leave to cool.

Mix in the tomato juice.

Divide the mixture into balls. This mixture makes about 30 walnut sized balls, but make them larger or smaller if you prefer. You may need extra oats if you make them any smaller. Roll each ball in the oats until it is evenly covered. Squeeze them to make the moisture permeate the oats and put to one side in a cool place for about 30 minutes.

Heat the deep fat until a small piece of bread turns golden in a few seconds. Fry about 4 or 5 balls at a time (depending on the size of your pan) until the coating is golden brown. Drain on kitchen paper and keep warm until all the balls have been fried.

Golden Marrow Bake

Serves 4–6

Delany's, Shrewsbury

1 large onion, chopped
4 large cloves garlic, crushed
1 large marrow, peeled, seeded and sliced
olive oil
2 teaspoons ground cumin
1 teaspoon ground coriander
½ teaspoon chilli powder
dash of cayenne pepper
2" (5cm) root of ginger, peeled and grated
1 small red pepper, seeded and chopped
1 small green pepper, seeded and chopped
12 oz (350g) sweetcorn
4 eggs, beaten
8 oz (225g) grated cheddar, plus a little extra for topping
juice of ½ lemon
salt and black pepper

Sauté the onion, garlic and sliced marrow in olive oil. After a couple of minutes add the spices and continue cooking until the marrow just begins to soften. Add the peppers and sweetcorn.

Mix in the beaten eggs, cheese and lemon juice and taste for seasoning, adding salt and black pepper to your satisfaction.

Place the mixture in an oven proof dish and sprinkle over a little more grated cheese. (A mixture of grated cheese and breadcrumbs will give a crisper topping.)

Bake at 350°F/180°C/Gas 4 for 15–20 minutes.

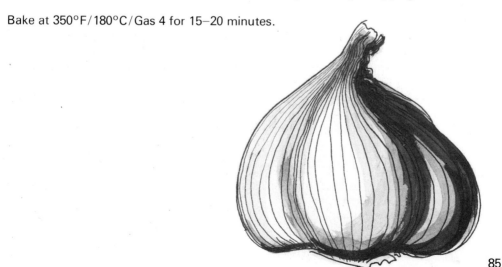

Stuffed Marrow

Henderson's Salad Table, Edinburgh
Chef; Nicholas Henderson

2 tablespoons oil
1 onion, sliced
2 cloves garlic, crushed
1 tablespoon mixed herbs
3 carrots, grated
3 parsnips, finely diced
1 swede, finely diced
1 red pepper, diced
2 sticks celery, finely sliced
4 oz (125g) mushrooms, sliced
salt and pepper
4 oz (125g) chopped mixed nuts
4 oz (125g) wholemeal breadcrumbs (approx.)
1 marrow about 12" (30cm) long
2 oz (50g) butter
2 oz (50g) wholemeal flour
1 pint (575ml) milk
2 tomatoes, finely sliced
chopped parsley

Sauté the onion, garlic and mixed herbs in the oil until soft. Add the carrot, parsnips and swede. When these vegetables are half cooked, add the pepper, celery and mushrooms. Cook until all the vegetables are tender.

Remove from the heat, season and add enough nuts and breadcrumbs to give a stiff mixture.

Cut the marrow in half lengthwise and scoop out the seeds. Cut into sections about 3" (8cm) long and blanch them until just soft.

Place the pieces of marrow in an ovenproof serving dish and pile the stuffing mixture into each marrow section, forming a rounded mound. The size of the mound will depend on how finely you chop the vegetables. Melt the butter in a pan, add the flour and cook for 1 minute, stirring constantly. Gradually add the milk, stirring all the time, and bring the sauce to the boil. Cook until the mixture thickens. Season.

Coat each piece of marrow with sauce and top with tomato slices. Bake at 400°F/200°C/Gas 6 for about 20 minutes, until golden on top and bubbling. Serve garnished with a sprinkling of parsley.

Mushroom Kasha with Stir-fry Sprouted Pulses and Brown Rice

Serves 4

Cook's Delight, Berkhamsted
Chef; Khaieng Tyler

8 oz (225g) brown rice

For the mushroom kasha:

8 oz (225g) organic mushrooms
1 oz (25g) dried shitake mushrooms
1 carrot
1 onion
6 oz (175g) kasha (roasted buckwheat)
1 tablespoon unrefined olive oil
1 teaspoon chopped fresh ginger
1 tablespoon tamari
sea salt to taste
1 pint (575ml) filtered water

For the sprouted pulses:

4 oz (125g) sprouted lentils
4 oz (125g) sprouted adukis
4 oz (125g) soya sprouts
2 cloves garlic
1 teaspoon chopped fresh sweet basil
1 leek
2 tablespoons unrefined sesame oil
1 tablespoon soya sauce
sea salt to taste

Wash the mushrooms and cut into ½" (1cm) pieces. Soak the shitake mushrooms in hot water for 30 minutes then slice into thin strips. Dice the carrot into ½" (1cm) cubes and blanch in a little salt water. Chop the onion finely. Wash the kasha, drain and dry roast. Set aside.

Heat a saucepan, add the oil and ginger, stir and add the onion. Cook until soft then add the kasha, mushrooms and carrot. Stir for a couple of minutes. Add the tamari and water, bring to the boil and simmer until all the water is absorbed.

Wash the rice well, drain and place in a pan. Cover with filtered water (one and a half times the volume of rice). Bring to the boil and simmer for 30–45 minutes until the rice is cooked.

Wash the sprouts well. Chop the garlic finely. Slice the leek into fine rings. Heat the oil in a wok, add the garlic and leek, stir fry for one minute, then add all the apricots. Toss thoroughly. Sprinkle in the basil and the soya sauce. Stir fry for two minutes (test for salt and add at this stage if required). Stir fry for another minute. Serve immediately.

Arrange the mushroom kasha, brown rice and stir-fried pulses together on a platter and serve hot.

Mushroom Moussaka

Cherry Orchard, London
Chef; Karola

3 medium aubergines, sliced ½″ (1cm) thick
salt
1 lb (450g) potatoes, peeled and sliced

For the mushroom sauce:

1 lb (450g) onions, sliced
oil
2 cloves garlic
1 lb (450g) mushrooms
2–3 sprigs fresh parsley, chopped
10 fl oz (275ml) tomato juice
2 tablespoons tomato paste
4 fl oz (125ml) wine vinegar
seasoning
2 oz (50g) breadcrumbs
8 oz (225g) cheese, grated
2 eggs, beaten

For the white sauce:

4 fl oz (125ml) oil
6 fl oz (175g) flour
½ stick cinnamon
1¼ pints (725ml) milk
pinch of salt and pepper
½ teaspoon nutmeg
2 medium eggs
2 oz (50g) breadcrumbs
4 oz (125g) grated cheese

Salt the aubergine slices lightly and leave in a colander for approximately half an hour until slightly moist. Drain, removing excess salt, and bake on an oiled tray in the oven at 350°F/180°C/Gas 4 for about 15 minutes, until tender.

Steam or boil the potatoes until tender.

Make the mushroom sauce. Lightly sauté the onions in oil until golden. Add the garlic. Slice the mushrooms and gently sauté with the onions and garlic. Add the chopped parsley, tomato juice, tomato paste and the wine vinegar. Season to taste. Leave to simmer until most of the liquid has been absorbed, then stir in the breadcrumbs, cheese and eggs. Remove from the heat and put to one side.

Make the white sauce. Heat the milk and cinnamon stick together in a pan. Warm the oil in a saucepan over a low flame, sprinkle in the flour, stirring briskly to avoid lumps to make a roux. When the milk has reached just below boiling point remove the cinnamon and whisk the milk into the roux. Stir continuously, heating until the sauce comes to the boil and thickens. Remove from the heat, beat in the eggs and season with salt, pepper and nutmeg.

Oil a medium casserole dish. Cover the bottom with sliced potatoes and half the aubergines. Pour over half the mushroom sauce, then the remaining aubergines and a final layer of mushroom sauce. Pour over the white sauce and sprinkle the top with breadcrumbs and grated cheese.

Cover with foil and bake on the middle shelf at 350°F/180°C/Gas 4 for 40 minutes. Remove the foil for the last 15 minutes of the cooking time.

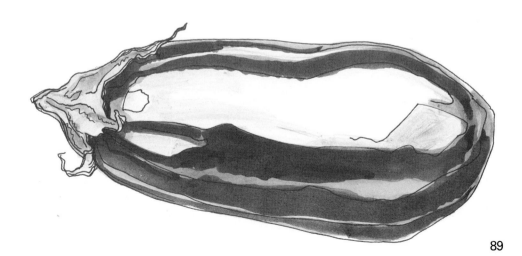

Savoury Mushroom Bake

The Old Bakehouse, Castle Cary
Chef; Carol Seeley

8 oz (225g) wholemeal breadcrumbs
4 oz (25g) mixed milled nuts
4 tablespoons sunflower oil
1 large onion
8 oz (225g) mushrooms
8 oz (225g) fresh or tinned tomatoes
salt and pepper
1 teaspoon dried marjoram

This recipe is ideal for Vegans.

Combine the breadcrumbs and nuts and fry them in 3 tablespoons of oil until golden.
A little extra oil may be needed depending on the absorbency of the breadcrumbs.
Set aside.

Chop the onion finely and sauté in remaining oil until transparent. Add the chopped
mushrooms, marjoram, seasoning and tomatoes (the tinned variety are particularly
suitable for keeping the mushroom layer moist). Simmer for 10 minutes.

In a lightly oiled ovenproof dish alternately layer the breadcrumbs and nut mixture with
the vegetables, starting and finishing with the breadcrumbs.

Bake in the oven for 30 minutes at 375°F/190°C/or Gas mark 5.

Nutty Cottage Pie

Herbs, Skipton
Chef; Joan Fikkert

1 onion, sliced
1 oz (25g) vegetable margarine
8 oz (225g) mixed nuts, finely chopped
4 oz (125g) wholemeal breadcrumbs
1 lb (450g) fresh tomatoes, skinned and chopped
pinch mixed herbs
5 floz (150ml) stock
½ teaspoon vegetable extract
2½ lb (1.4 kg) mashed potato
1 oz (25g) grated cheese
salt and pepper

Fry the onions in the margarine until soft. Stir in the nuts and the breadcrumbs, tomatoes and herbs and cook for another 10 minutes.

Stir in the stock and vegetable extract and pour into an ovenproof dish.

Carefully spread the potato over the nut mixture, making sure it is totally covered then sprinkle over the grated cheese.

Bake at 375°F/190°C/Gas 5 for 30 minutes until the potato has turned a golden brown colour.

Parsnip and Sweetcorn Lattice Pie

Serves 4–6

Rainbow's End, Glastonbury
Chef; Shelagh Spear

For the pastry:

8 oz (225g) wholemeal flour
4 oz (125g) soft vegetable margarine
½ teaspoon salt
½ teaspoon baking powder
water to mix
2 oz (50g) additional butter or margarine for a richer pastry (optional)

For the filling:

1 ½ oz (35g) butter
1 medium onion, finely chopped
12 oz (350g) young parsnips, grated
1 tablespoon freshly chopped parsley
4 fl oz (125ml) evaporated milk
12 oz (350g) tin sweetcorn, drained of liquid
salt and pepper
2 eggs
sesame seeds to decorate
chopped parsley to serve

Many recipes using parsnips tend to mask their flavour. What I have tried to do in this recipe is to enhance their sweetness with other ingredients. To balance the overall taste we serve it with a fiery horseradish sauce.

Prepare the pastry. Seive together the flour, salt and baking powder. Rub the fat into the flour and then gradually add enough water to form a smooth dough. If you prefer a richer pastry add extra fat by rolling out the pastry, spreading it with daubs of fat, folding the buttered sides together and re-rolling; that is, in the style of rough puff pastry. Leave to rest.

Make the filling. Melt the butter in a thick bottomed saucepan, add the onion and sweat it until translucent. Add the grated parsnips and continue to cook over a low heat, with the lid on. Avoid colouring by stirring it then replacing the lid. When the parsnips are soft, remove the pan from the heat and add the other ingredients; parsley, evaporated milk, sweetcorn, seasoning and eggs. (Save a little egg yolk as egg wash for the pastry.)

92

Line a 10″ (25cm) quiche dish (preferably metal) with pastry. Use the minimum to give a thin layer. Pile in the filling. Roll out the remaining pastry and cut into ½″ (1cm) strips. Use these to make a lattice top for the pie. Brush the strips with egg wash and sprinkle them with sesame seeds. Bake at 400°F/200°C/Gas 6 for 40 minutes, until golden brown and crisp. Serve hot sprinkled with finely chopped fresh parsley.

Pasta, Spinach and Cashew Nut Bake   *Serves 4*

Gannets, Newark
Chef; Hilary Bower

8 oz (225g) wholewheat pasta spirals
1 lb (450g) cooked spinach, roughly chopped
4 medium leeks, cleaned, sliced and quickly sautéed in a little butter
4 oz (125g) cashew nuts
8 oz (225g) cottage or cream cheese

For the sauce:

1 ½ oz (35g) butter
1 ½ oz (35g) plain flour
1 pint (575ml) milk
salt and pepper
freshly grated nutmeg
2 oz (50g) Parmesan cheese, freshly grated if possible

Cook the pasta as directed on the packet. Rinse in cold water and drain well.

In a large bowl mix together the pasta, spinach, leeks, cashew nuts and cottage cheese, stirring well to make sure all the ingredients are evenly distributed.

Make the sauce. Melt the butter, add the flour and cook for one or two minutes. Remove the pan from the heat and gradually add all the milk. Return to the heat and continue to cook until thickened, stirring all the time. Season with salt and pepper and a generous grating of nutmeg. Taste and season again as necessary.

Add two thirds of the sauce to the pasta mixture and mix well. Put this mixture into an oven proof dish and top with the remainder of the sauce and the Parmesan. Bake at 375°F/190°C/Gas 5 for 25–30 minutes or until brown on top.

Peacock Pie

Hockneys, Croydon
Chef; Paul Keeler

4 oz (25g) black eyed beans, soaked overnight
2 oz (50g) cashew nuts
5 oz (150g) coconut cream
12 oz (350g) onion, chopped
olive oil
1 dessertspoon dill weed
1 tablespoon yellow mustard seeds
2 tablespoons chopped coriander leaves
salt and pepper
lemon juice (about 1 tablespoon)

For the topping:

12 oz (350g) cauliflower (1 medium head)
1 lb (450g) fresh tomatoes
3 oz (75g) Cheddar cheese, grated
dob of butter
salt and pepper

This dish is named after a poetry anthology by Walter De la Mare.

Make the filling. Cook the black eyed beans until soft, adding a little salt for the last five minutes of the cooking time.

Roast the cashews lightly in a medium oven, 350°F/180°C/Gas 4.

Melt the coconut cream over a low flame or in the oven. Beware, it burns easily.

Sauté the onions in olive oil, adding the dill and mustard seeds. When the onions are soft add the coriander and cook for a little longer.

Add salt, pepper and lemon juice to taste, remove from the heat and stir in the beans, cashews and coconut. Put to one side.

Make the topping. Boil the cauliflower in salted water until soft. Drain.

Skin the tomatoes by plunging them into boiling water for a few seconds and then transferring them straight to a bowl of cold water. This helps remove the skins more easily without actually cooking them.

Mix all the topping ingredients together and either purée or mash.

Place the filling in a greased baking dish, cover with the topping and heat through, covered, at 350°F/180°C/Gas 4 for about half an hour or until hot.

Pine Nutmeat en Croûte with Chasseur Sauce or Cranberry and Apple Sauce

Serves 6–8

Herbs, Coventry
Chef; Robert Jackson

For the nutmeat:

1 oz (25g) butter
1 medium onion, finely chopped
8 oz (225g) pine nut kernels
4 oz (125g) fresh white breadcrumbs
2 eggs, beaten
salt and black pepper
grated nutmeg
3 tablespoons milk (approx.)

For the pastry:

8 oz (225g) wholemeal flour
4 oz (125g) butter or margarine
1 egg, beaten
water to mix

For the stuffing:

2 oz (50g) butter, ice cold
6 oz (175g) wholemeal breadcrumbs
grated rind and juice of 1 lemon
½ teaspoon marjoram
½ teaspoon thyme
1 dessertspoon chopped parsley
salt and black pepper

Prepare the nutmeat. Melt the butter in a saucepan and add the onion, fry until soft. Add all the other ingredients with just enough milk to achieve a firm consistency.

Prepare the pastry. Rub the fat into the flour until the mix resembles fine breadcrumbs. Add the beaten egg and enough cold water to form a smooth dough. Leave to rest for an hour.

Prepare the stuffing. Rub the butter into the breadcrumbs. Add all the other ingredients and mix well.

Assemble the dish. Roll the pastry into a rectangle about the size of a Swiss roll tin – or a little larger if you can manage it. Mould the nutmeat into a loaf shape. Lay the stuffing down the centre of the pastry and place the loaf on top. Brush some beaten egg around the edge of the pastry and roll up, sealing the ends firmly. Lay the loaf on a lightly greased baking tray, join side down. Brush beaten egg all over the surface and use any surplus pastry as decoration, cut into shapes such as leaves, flowers or holly. Use more egg to fix the shapes into place and add a final brush of egg for glaze.

Bake for about 30 minutes at 375°F/190°C/Gas 5 until golden. Leave to rest for 10 minutes before transferring to an attractive serving dish. Carve as required in generous slices accompanied by the Chasseur or Cranberry and Apple sauces.

For the chasseur sauce:

3 tablespoons vegetable oil
1 medium onion, finely diced
6 oz (175g) button mushrooms, sliced
4 fl oz (125ml) white wine
½ pint (275ml) water
1 vegetable stock cube
14 oz (400g) tinned tomatoes, chopped
1 teaspoon tarragon
salt and black pepper
1 tablespoon cornflour to thicken (approx.)

Heat the oil and sauté the onion until soft. Add the mushrooms and cook for a further 2 minutes. Add the white wine and boil briskly for 2 minutes.

Add all the other ingredients excluding the cornflour. Bring to the boil and simmer for about 10 minutes. Thicken slightly with cornflour and check the seasoning.

For the fresh cranberry and apple sauce:

2 tablespoons oil
1 medium leek, cleaned and chopped
1 medium onion, chopped
2 medium carrots, washed and chopped
2 medium cooking apples, chopped
1 lb (450g) fresh cranberries, finely minced
¼ pint (150ml) red wine
1 pint (575ml) water
14 oz (400g) tinned tomatoes

½ teaspoon mixed herbs
salt and black pepper
1 tablespoon sugar (optional)

Heat the oil in a large saucepan and add all the chopped vegetables and apples. Sauté for a few minutes until lightly coloured. Add half the minced cranberries with all the red wine, water, tomatoes and mixed herbs. Bring to the boil, cover and simmer for about 45 minutes.

Add the rest of the cranberries and simmer gently for 2–3 minutes. Season and adjust consistency with water if necessary. Add sugar if necessary.

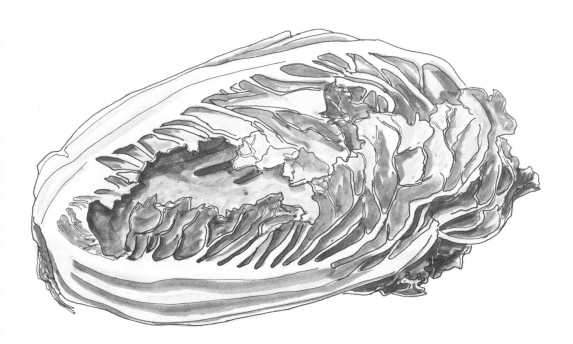

Pizza Pie

Serves 6

Nature's Way, Eastbourne
Chefs; Dorothy and Maurice Fossitt

For the base:

1½ oz (37g) vegetarian margarine
6 oz (175g) 85% wholemeal self-raising flour
3 level teaspoons baking powder
small pinch black pepper
1 good pinch sea salt
3–4 tablespoons water

For the topping:

1 lb (450g) onions, sliced and sautéed in a little oil until soft
8 oz (225g) fresh tomatoes, sliced
6 oz (175g) carrots, grated and blanched
4 oz (125g) peas, cooked
8 oz (225g) courgettes, blanched

For the nutty topping:

1 oz (25g) flaked almonds
1 oz (25g) wheatgerm
4 oz (125g) grated cheese

Make the base. Rub the margarine and flour together. Add the baking powder and seasoning and gradually add the water until a fairly soft dough is formed. Knead lightly on a floured board and then roll into a 9" (23cm) circle. Place on a greased baking sheet and leave to rest in a cold place for 30 minutes.

Prepare all the topping ingredients. Spread the onions over the dough circle, followed by the tomatoes, carrots, peas and finally the courgettes making sure they spread right to the edge.

Make the nutty topping by mixing together the three ingredients until they resemble a crumble and then sprinkle over the courgettes. Again make sure the mixture reaches right to the edge.

Place in a pre-heated oven at 400°F/200°C/Gas 6 for 25–30 minutes.

98

Gerard's Rice

Cheese Press, Crickhowell
Chef; Mrs Morgan-Grenville

2 large onions, finely sliced
3 oz (75g) butter
4 oz (125g) mushrooms, halved or quartered if they are large
8 oz (225g) fresh tomatoes, skinned and chopped
1 lb (450g) cooked potatoes (steamed if possible)
1 banana, thickly sliced
1 apple, cored and sliced
2 oz (50g) raisins or sultanas
1 teaspoon tabasco
1 tablespoon curry paste (optional)
5 fl oz (150ml) natural yoghurt
8 oz (225g) cooked brown rice (or more if you are hungry), kept hot
8 oz (225g) Cheddar cheese, grated

Fry the onions in butter until soft. Add the mushrooms and tomatoes, then stir. Add the potatoes, cut into large dice, banana, apple, and raisins. Stir and simmer gently for a few minutes.

Add the tabasco and curry paste (if using it) and the cheese, and simmer for about 15 minutes, until the vegetables are tender and the flavours amalgamated. Add a little water during the cooking if the mixture seems a little dry.

Just before serving, stir in the yoghurt. Serve on a bed of brown rice.

Jamaican Run Down

Serves 4–6

Huckleberry's, Bath
Chef; Wendy Mathews

5 oz (150g) creamed coconut
1 pint (575ml) water
2 carrots, cut into 1" (2.5cm) cubes
1 green pepper, sliced
1 onion, sliced
1 bay leaf
1 ½ teaspoons thyme, or a couple of sprigs
2 cloves garlic, chopped
1 chilli, chopped
1 medium size potato, cubed
1 parsnip, cubed
1 small sweet potato, cubed
8 oz (225g) kidney beans, soaked and cooked
soy sauce
salt and pepper

In Jamaica this recipe traditionally uses milk by soaking freshly grated coconut in hot water, and extracting the juice. However, the use of creamed coconut is just as effective and makes the process simpler.

Put the creamed coconut in a pan with the water, and bring to the boil. The coconut will eventually melt and the oil separate out. When this happens, add the carrot, pepper and onion. Let the mixture boil for 10 minutes and then add the potatoes, bay leaf, thyme, garlic and chilli.

Once the potatoes have softened a little add the parsnip and sweet potato. Add the kidney beans last of all, when the vegetables are almost done. Season with soy sauce and salt and pepper.

By the end of the cooking process the majority of the liquid should have disappeared. The vegetables should be soft but not mushy, and swathed in a coat of creamy coconut. In order to achieve this it may be necessary to adjust the water content by boiling vigorously so that the excess water may evaporate, or by adding extra water if it looks as though the liquid may all evaporate before the vegetables are ready.

Serve immediately on a bed of brown rice.

100

Sambal

Sree Krishna, London
Chef; Mr Ramanarayan

1 lb (450g) toor dall (pigeon peas)
½ teaspoon turmeric
1 oz (25g) coriander seeds
15 dried red chillies (add fewer for a less fiery effect)
15 curry leaves
2 teaspoons desiccated coconut
½ teaspoon fenugreek seeds
⅛ teaspoon asafetida powder
1 teaspoon tamarind concentrate dissolved in 5 fl oz (150ml) water
4 okra (ladies' fingers) or 1 small aubergine cut into chunks or 3 carrots, diced
2 tomatoes
2 onions

For the garnish:

1 teaspoon fenugreek seeds
3 curry leaves
1 red chilli
1 teaspoon black mustard seeds
oil
seasoning

This is a dish from the south of India where they specialise in a rather fiery vegetarian cuisine. All these ingredients can be easily obtained from your local Indian grocer or health food store.

Wash the dall and cook with salt and the turmeric until it is soft and fairly liquid.

Meanwhile prepare the spices. Roughly grind the coriander seeds then fry in oil with the chillies, curry leaves, coconut, fenugreek seeds and asafetida powder. When the chillies begin to darken remove from the heat and place the mixture in a liquidiser with enough water to make a paste. Set aside.

Chop the vegetables cutting the tomatoes into quarters and halving the onions, add this to the cooked dall and simmer until the vegetables are almost done. Pour in the tamarind water and the spiced paste and cook for a further 15 minutes.

In a frying pan heat some oil and gently fry the fenugreek seeds, mustard seeds, curry leaves and roughly chopped red chilli. After a few minutes add this to the Sambal. Serve hot with rice or Indian bread.

Savoury Parcels

Serves 4

That Café, Manchester
Chef; Joseph Quinn

8 oz (225g) green bell peppers
8 oz (225g) red bell peppers
12 oz (350g) mushrooms
12 oz (350g) onions
olive oil, for frying
3 cloves of garlic, peeled and crushed
12 oz (350g) puff pastry
4 tomatoes, sliced
4 oz (125g) grated Cheddar cheese
1 egg for glazing

Finely chop the peppers, mushrooms and onions and sauté in a little olive oil until sealed, but still crisp — about 5 minutes. Add the garlic, stir fry for 1 minute and remove from the heat. Place the mixture in a colander to drain. Leave until cold.

Roll the pastry on a floured board into 4 squares about 6" (15cm) square. In the centre of each pastry square spoon one quarter of the filling, top with tomato slices and cheese. Join the pastry corner to corner into the centre and pinch the edges firmly together to form a parcel. Place the parcels on floured or a lightly greased baking sheet, glaze with egg and bake at 425°F/220°C/Gas 7 for about 15 minutes until golden brown.

Delicious served with a green salad. If you should have too much filling for the four parcels either freeze the excess for another time or serve separately with the cooked parcels.

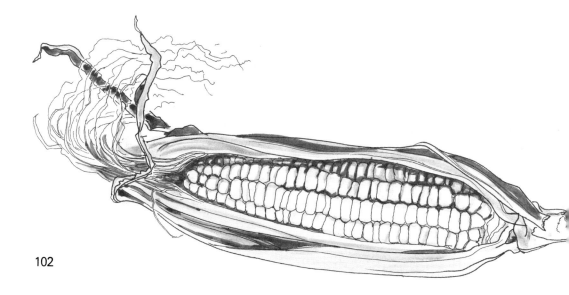

Roulade of Spinach and Pistachio Kernels with Dijon Mustard Sauce

Serves 4

Food For Thought, London
Chef; Siriporn Duncan

4 oz (125g) fresh spinach, cooked, drained and squeezed of ALL excess water
1 oz (25g) butter
salt and freshly milled black pepper
2 oz (50g) shelled pistachio nuts, finely chopped

Sauté the spinach in butter for a few minutes, season with salt and pepper, add pistachios and set aside.

Whisk egg whites with salt and pepper until stiff, then fold into the spinach mixture carefully.

Spread the mixture onto a swiss roll tin lined with greaseproof paper. Bake in a pre-heated oven at 375°F/190°C/Gas 5 for approximately 15 minutes.

As soon as the sponge is cooked, turn it out of the tin, peel away the greaseproof paper and roll it up. Cut into 12 thin slices.

For the Dijon mustard sauce:

8 shallots, thinly sliced
2 cloves garlic, crushed
2 oz (50g) butter
4 fl oz (125ml) single cream
salt and freshly milled pepper
2 heaped teaspoons Dijon mustard, or more if preferred

Sauté garlic and shallots gently in the butter until soft.

Add the mustard and cook for 1 minute longer.

Remove from the heat, liquidize, return to the heat and bring to the boil, after adding the cream.

Season with salt and pepper.

Spinach and Fetta Cheese Pie

Serves 6–8

Guild Café, Bristol

1 lb (450g) shortcrust pastry made with wholemeal flour
3 lb (1½kg) fresh spinach
1 large onion, chopped
4 oz (125g) butter
3 cloves garlic, crushed
¼ teaspoon nutmeg, grated
salt and pepper
8 oz (225g) fetta cheese
2 tablespoons sesame seeds

This dish is also extremely appetizing made with frozen puff pastry or filo pastry and frozen spinach, making it a very superior convenience food.

Make the pastry and leave to rest.

Wash the spinach thoroughly, removing any rough stalks. Press into a large saucepan containing about 1" (2.5cm) boiling salted water. Cook for about 15 minutes, stirring at frequent intervals. The quantity should reduce drastically.

Drain well, then chop the spinach finely, or purée in a liquidizer or food processor. Be careful not to process it so much that it loses its texture.

Soften the onion in the butter, then add the spinach, garlic, nutmeg, salt and pepper. Stir well and continue cooking until all the butter has been absorbed. Crumble in the fetta cheese.

Line a large pie dish with half the pastry and bake blind for 15 minutes at 375°F/190°C/Gas 5.

Once the pastry base is cooked fill it with the spinach mixture. Make a top with the remaining pastry, brush over with egg or milk and sprinkle with sesame seeds. Bake at 350°F/180°C/Gas 4 until crisp.

Tagliatelli con Chianti

Food For Thought, London
Chef; Kit Norman

1 lb (450g) fresh spinach tagliatelli
salt
olive oil
3 cloves garlic, crushed
1 lb (450g) button mushrooms, thickly sliced
pepper
tamari
1 small onion, finely chopped
a little butter for frying
1 stick celery, finely chopped
1 small carrot, grated
1 rounded dessertspoon wholewheat flour
a pinch of thyme
1 dessertspoon tomato purée
1 tin Italian peeled plum tomatoes
2 cups vegetable stock or hot water
2 cups good Chianti
½ teaspoon basil
½ teaspoon marjoram
1 heaped teaspoon oregano
½ – ¾ lb (225–350g) fresh, young spinach
1 handful parsley, finely chopped
1 lb (450g) mozzarella cheese, thinly sliced
1 heaped tablespoon grated Parmesan cheese

Cook pasta in plenty of water (to which has been added a little salt and olive oil), for 5 minutes. Drain, rinse and toss in a little olive oil.

Fry the garlic gently in olive oil for 1 minute, then add mushrooms and fry until just cooked. Season with basil, salt and pepper and a splash of tamari. Drain and reserve any liquid.

Fry the onion in butter for a few minutes, then add the celery and carrot and cook until soft.

Stir in flour and thyme and cook over a low heat for a few minutes.

Add tomato purée, reserved mushroom juices and the juice from the tinned tomatoes. Add enough stock to make a sauce of medium consistency.

Cook gently for a few minutes, then add the wine and simmer for 5 minutes.

Sprinkle over the herbs, salt and pepper and cook for a further 3 minutes. The sauce should be rather thin and strongly flavoured as the pasta will absorb both moisture and flavour.

Wash spinach thoroughly and pack tightly into a saucepan, cover and cook for 5–10 minutes. Take care not to overcook. Drain, and rinse well, pressing out excess moisture. Chop spinach and mix in parsley.

Roughly chop tomatoes, then thoroughly combine all the ingredients except the cheeses. Check and adjust the seasoning.

Place the mixture in a greased oven-proof baking dish. Cut the tagliatelli with a sharp knife if necessary, this will aid serving.

Top with mozzarella and Parmesan and bake in a medium hot oven for 25 – 30 minutes.

Tofu à la Crème

Wild Oats II, Bristol
Chef; Nicky Smith

1 block oak smoked tofu and 1 block plain tofu (or 2 blocks plain tofu)

For the marinade:

¼ bottle red wine
¼ bottle white wine
½ cup shoyu
2 large cloves of garlic

For the tofu – cashewnut cream:

⅓ block plain tofu
⅔ packet unsweetened soya milk
8 oz (225g) cashewnuts
18 fl oz (500ml) unrefined sunflower oil

For the casserole:

oil for sautéeing
3 medium onions, chopped
12 small courgettes, sliced
1 lb (450g) button mushrooms, halve the large ones
1 tablespoon paprika
1 tablespoon fresh parsley
½ tablespoon rosemary
1 teaspoon basil
1 teaspoon marjoram
1 teaspoon oregano
1 teaspoon thyme
shoyu, to taste
black pepper, to taste

Chop the smoked tofu and two thirds of the remaining blocks of plain tofu into ½"
(1cm) square cubes (set aside the other section for the tofu and cashewnut cream).

Place the cubes in an ovenproof dish and add the marinade ingredients. Marinate for as
long as possible — overnight is ideal. If, however, you wish to prepare the dish at short
notice it is as effective to cook the tofu cubes in the marinade in a very low oven for an
hour or so while you prepare the rest of the dish.

Poach the remaining third of the block of tofu in plain water until it floats, then blend it
in a liquidiser until pulverised.

Add the soya milk and cashew nuts and blend them for several minutes until the
mixture is reasonably smooth. Then add the sunflower oil slowly — as for mayonnaise
— until the sauce thickens.

Heat some deep frying oil and fry the tofu cubes, a few at a time, until crisp and
golden. Drain on kitchen towel. If you prefer, you can shallow fry the tofu cubes in a
very hot oil in a heavy pan. Ensure that you stir vigorously so that the water does not
escape from the tofu and cause it to fall apart.

In a little oil (preferably unrefined corn-germ oil for flavour), sauté the vegetables. Start
with the onion, cooking until it begins to brown, then the courgettes, followed a
minute or so later by the mushrooms, stirring well all the time over a high heat. When
the vegetables begin to sweat add the paprika, herbs and a dash of shoyu. They will be
very receptive to flavourings at this point, and the shoyu will seal in the flavours.

Add the cashewnut cream and the marinade. Stir well and season. Add a little
arrowroot if the sauce is too runny. Simmer for 10 minutes longer until the vegetables
are cooked but still crunchy and colourful. Stir in the tofu cubes and serve
accompanied by the leftover wine.

Tofu and Mushroom Goulash

Serves 4

York Wholefood, York
Chef; Peter Graves

1 large or two small onions, finely chopped
2 cloves garlic, crushed
olive oil
1 lb (450g) mushrooms
14 oz (400g) tin of tomatoes
8 oz (225g) firm tofu
cayenne pepper to taste
salt to taste
1 red pepper, sliced
1 handful chopped parsley

Cook the finely chopped onion and crushed garlic in oil in a saucepan until the onion is translucent. Add the mushrooms, broken into pieces, stir and cook for a few minutes.

Roughly chop the tomatoes and add to the pan with their juice. Add the cubed tofu with the cayenne pepper and salt. Cook on a low heat for 15 minutes, then add the sliced pepper and cook for a further 15–20 minutes, by which time the sauce should have reduced and thickened.

Throw in the chopped parsley, stir and serve immediately on a bed of rice or with new potatoes.

Vegetables in Garlic Sauce

Serves 6

Arnolfini, Bristol

3–4 lb (approx. 1.5kg) mixed vegetables including carrots, parsnips, turnips,
  cauliflowers, mushrooms and peppers
3 oz (75g) margarine
6–8 cloves of garlic, crushed
3 oz (75g) flour
1 ½ pints (875ml) milk, warmed
salt and pepper

Prepare all the vegetables and cut into equal sized pieces. Cook in boiling water until just tender.

Melt the margarine in a pan, add the garlic and stir in the flour. Cook to a golden brown; then, over a low heat, gradually add the milk, stirring, until it thickens. Season to taste.

Place the vegetables in an ovenproof dish and cover with the sauce. Bake at 350°F/180°C/Gas 4 for about 20 minutes until golden brown and bubbling.

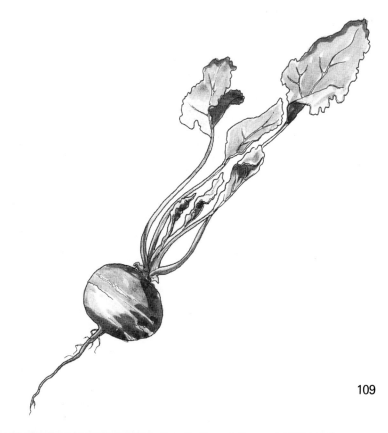

Vegetables in Korma Sauce

Serves 4

Food For Health, London
Chef; Abdel Mansoir Rahman

¼ teaspoon saffron threads
1 tablespoon poppy seeds
piece of cinnamon stick or 1 teaspoon powdered cinnamon
2–3 seeded small green chillis or ½ teaspoon cayenne pepper
1 teaspoon ground cumin
1 teaspoon coriander seeds
½ teaspoon freshly ground black pepper
1 teaspoon salt
1 clove garlic
2–3 tablespoons water
6 tablespoons vegetable oil
10 cardamom pods
10 cloves
1 onion, chopped
some 85% wholemeal flour
1–2 tablespoons lemon juice
10 oz (275g) natural yoghurt
2 oz (50g) cashew nuts
parsley or coriander to garnish

This delicious sauce is suitable to serve with a selection of any vegetables in season.
Mixtures of broccoli, cauliflower, peas and carrots or green beans, potatoes, leeks and
mushrooms are two particularly good selections. Just try to make sure that the
vegetables are not too watery and that they are cooked until only just tender.

Soak the saffron in 4 fl oz (125ml) boiling water and leave for about 2 hours.

Prepare your vegetables and cook until slightly tender. Place in an ovenproof dish in
the oven. Turn the oven on to 350°F/180°C/Gas 4.

Place in a blender the poppy seeds, cinnamon, chillis, cumin, coriander, pepper, salt,
garlic, ginger and blend to a paste adding a little water if necessary. If you do not have
a blender use a pestle and mortar.

Heat the oil in a pan and cook the onion without browning for 4–5 minutes. Stir in the
blended paste, cardamoms and cloves and cook for another minute or two. Stir in a
little flour, enough to make a slack roux. Add the saffron water, lemon juice and
yoghurt and bring to the boil. If the sauce becomes very stiff add a little vegetable
water, but do not make the sauce runny. The name Korma means dry and the sauce is
just there to give flavour and a coating to the vegetables. Taste the sauce and adjust
the flavour if necessary. (You can make the sauce without using the flour.)

110

Pour the sauce over the vegetables and cook, uncovered, in the oven for 30–40 minutes. Stir in the cashew nuts, and if the vegetables are very dry add more yoghurt, cream or vegetable stock. Return to the oven for another 10 minutes.

Garnish with parsley or coriander and serve with brown rice.

Stir Fry Rice and Vegetables

Serves 4

Neal's Yard Bakery, London
Chef; Rachel Haigh

1 medium onion
2 medium carrots
1 green pepper
1 tablespoon soya oil or 1 oz (25g) butter
½ teaspoon cardamom seeds
4 oz (125g) tomatoes
2 cloves garlic, crushed
1 egg
8 oz (225g) brown rice, cooked
1 tablespoon tamari
1 tablespoon tahini
freshly ground black pepper
freshly chopped parsley or coriander to garnish

Slice the onion into thin rings, slice the carrots and green pepper into long thin strips.

Heat the oil or butter in a wok or large frying pan. Add the sliced onion and carrots. Stir fry for 2–3 minutes.

Grind the cardamom seeds as finely as possible with a pestle and mortar. Add to the wok with the green pepper.

Cut the tomatoes into small pieces and add to the wok with the crushed garlic. Stir fry for another 5 minutes.

Break the egg into the wok and stir vigorously as it cooks.

Add the rice, tamari, tahini and ground black pepper. Stir fry for a further 5 minutes or until the rice has heated through. Serve immediately with a sprinkling of freshly chopped parsley or coriander.

Sweet and Sour Stir Fried Vegetables

Serves 4

Everyman Bistro, Liverpool

3 tablespoons (45ml) vegetable oil
2 cloves garlic, crushed
1 medium onion, finely chopped
1 medium carrot, finely sliced
2 medium red or green peppers, seeded and cut into strips
8 oz (225g) white cabbage, finely shredded
6 radishes, sliced
6 oz (175g) beansprouts, washed, drained
2 tablespoons rice or cider vinegar
2 tablespoons clear honey
2 tablespoons soya sauce, or more if you prefer

The stir fried vegetables are only lightly cooked in this Chinese inspired recipe and should retain some crunch. This dish is quick to prepare and very tasty. Serve with boiled rice.

Heat the oil in a wok, saucepan or frying pan and add the garlic, onion, carrot and pepper. Stir fry over a medium heat for 3–4 minutes. Add the cabbage and stir fry for another 3 minutes.

Add the radishes and beansprouts and stir fry for a further minute.

In a bowl mix the vinegar, honey and soya sauce. Pour the mixture on to the vegetables, stir briefly and serve immediately.

This dish can also be served cold as a salad. If you like ginger, try adding 2 teaspoons chopped fresh ginger when you fry the onion and garlic.

West Country Hot Pot

Food For Thought, London
Chef; Kit Norman

12 oz (350g) butterbeans, soaked overnight
1 teaspoon English mustard powder
1 teaspoon paprika
1 teaspoon ground coriander
¼ teaspoon ground ginger
1 rounded dessertspoon of butter or margarine
1 small onion, finely chopped
2 cloves garlic, crushed
1 rounded dessertspoon of wholewheat flour
a pinch of thyme
1 pint (575ml) medium sweet cider
3 medium courgettes, cut into bite-sized pieces
a little oil
8 oz (225g) button mushrooms
4 sticks celery, chopped
1 red pepper, chopped
1 green pepper, chopped
salt and pepper
½ teaspoon basil
5 fl oz (150ml) apple juice concentrate

Rinse the beans and cover with water. Boil for 45 minutes, or until nearly soft.

Stir in mustard, paprika, coriander and ginger and continue simmering until beans are cooked. Drain and reserve the stock.

Fry the onion and garlic gently for 3 minutes in the butter, then add the flour and thyme and cook for 3 more minutes over a low heat.

Gradually stir in some of the bean stock until the sauce is thick, then add the cider and simmer for 5 minutes.

Lightly fry the courgettes in oil and set aside. Fry mushrooms until they release their juices, then add the celery. After a few minutes add the peppers and heat through.

Check and adjust the seasoning, add a little basil.

Combine all the ingredients and enhance the flavour if necessary with apple juice concentrate. Simmer for 5–10 minutes and serve.

Wheat and Lentil Hotpot

Serves 6

Nuthouse, London
Chef; Abraham Nasr

4 oz (125g) margarine
4 oz (125g) onion, chopped
2 teaspoons tomato purée
4 oz (125g) carrot, cooked and chopped
4 oz (125g) potato, cooked and chopped
8 oz (225g) wheat, pre-cooked
8 oz (225g) lentils, pre-cooked
1 teaspoon basil
1 teaspoon ground cumin
salt and pepper
8 oz (225g) mushrooms, sliced
8 oz (225g) red or green pepper, chopped
1 pint (575ml) white sauce
4 oz (125g) Cheddar cheese, grated

Lightly fry the onion in the margarine, then add the tomato purée and about half a cup of water.

Add the carrot, potato, wheat, lentils and herbs and spices. Heat through and then pile into an ovenproof dish. Cover with mushrooms and pepper and pour over the white sauce. Any excess sauce may be served separately. Sprinkle over the cheese and place in a hot oven 400°F/200°C/Gas 6 for 10–15 minutes until hot and bubbly.

# Sweets

Karin's Apple Cake

Marno's, Ipswich
Chef; Penny

3 large eggs
6 oz (175g) demerara or raw golden granulated sugar
2 medium apples
8 oz (225g) 85% self-raising flour
2 tablespoons extra demerara sugar
2 oz (50g) chopped nuts
cinnamon, powdered, to taste

Preheat the oven to 350°F/180°C/Gas 4. Grease a 10" (25cm) sponge tin and line with paper.

Beat the eggs and sugar together in an electric mixer until very thick. While the eggs are beating, peel the apples, cut into quarters, remove pips and core, then slice finely into lengthwise wedges.

Sieve the flour over the egg and sugar mixture, then fold in very gently until thoroughly mixed. Pour this mixture into the prepared sponge tin. Stick the apple slices into the sponge at a slight angle, arranging them in concentric circles until the sponge is covered. Sprinkle over the extra sugar, nuts, and finally sprinkle with cinnamon to taste. Bake until risen and firm — about 20—25 minutes.

The same topping can be used on a Victoria sponge base, which, if served warm with cream or home-made custard, makes an excellent pudding.

Teisen Afal

Serves 6

Cnapan, Newport
Chef; Eluned Lloyd

4 oz (125g) margarine
4 oz (125g) soft brown sugar
2 eggs
rind and juice of 1 lemon
8 oz (225g) wholemeal self-raising flour
1 teaspoon cinnamon
4 eating apples
Honey or golden syrup to serve

This is a very popular Welsh dish which disappears quickly in our restaurant.

Butter a dish — I like a square or oblong shape best. A small loaf tin will do.

Cream together the margarine and sugar. Add the eggs with the lemon juice and rind. Fold in the flour and cinnamon. This will be a fairly stiff consistency. Put the mixture in the tin.

Core and slice the apples. Press the apple slices all over the top of the sponge mixture, packing as many as possible on. Flick a little water over the top.

Bake at 350°F/180°C/Gas 4 for about 50 minutes.

Serve with honey or golden syrup whilst still hot, although it is delicious eaten cold too.

Apricot and Banana Fool

Neal's Yard Bakery, London
Chef; Rachel Haigh

1 ½ fl oz (40ml) apricots, fresh or dried, cooked
2 bananas
½ pint (275ml) soya milk
pinch of nutmeg
pinch of ginger
pinch of cinnamon
2 oz (50g) flaked almonds

A vegan dish that will delight everyone's taste buds.

Blend all the ingredients except the almonds in a liquidiser or food processor until it is fairly smooth.

Pour into a bowl or four individual glasses and chill in the refrigerator for a few hours.

Just before serving sprinkle over the flaked almonds.

Apricot Slice

Nuthouse, London
Chef; Abraham Nasr

For the crumble:

6 oz (175g) wholemeal flour
3 oz (75g) medium oats
8 oz (225g) mixed chopped nuts
1 teaspoon mixed spice
1 teaspoon cinnamon
4 oz (125g) margarine
4 teaspoons concentrated apple juice

For the filling:

1 lb (450g) dried apricots, soaked overnight and then liquidised
8 oz (225g) raisins, soaked overnight

Place the flour, oats, nuts, cinnamon and spice in a large bowl and rub in the margarine. Add the apple juice and a little of the water in which the raisins were soaked and mix until it resembles fine breadcrumbs.

Grease a shallow baking tin with margarine. Place half the crumble evenly over the bottom, cover with apricots and raisins and finally the remaining crumble.

Bake at 375°F/190°C/Gas 5 for about 40 minutes.

Banana and Yoghurt Pie

Serves 6

Hockney's, Croydon
Chef; Paul Keeler

For the shortcrust pastry:

6 oz (175g) wholewheat flour
4 oz (125g) butter
3 oz (75g) dark brown sugar
1 tablespoon water
1 teaspoon cinnamon

For the filling:

3 large ripe bananas
4 eggs
8 fl oz (225ml) yoghurt
8 oz (225g) cottage cheese
6 oz (175g) honey
5 oz (150g) desiccated coconut
1 dessertspoon vanilla essence
2 dessertspoons lemon juice

This sweet is delicious eaten hot or cold.

Make the pastry using the quantities given, by your favourite method. Place in the fridge for at least 30 minutes.

Line a 10″ (25cm) flan case with the pastry and bake blind for 10 minutes at 400°F/200°C/Gas 6.

Liquidise all the filling ingredients together until smooth.

Pour the filling into the pastry case and bake at 350°F/180°C/Gas 4 for 30 minutes or until the top is golden.

That Café's Banana Pudding

Serves 6

That Café, Manchester
Chef; Joseph Quinn

4 bananas
juice of ½ lemon
juice of 1 orange
6 oz (175g) fresh wholemeal breadcrumbs
4 oz (125g) brown sugar
approx. ¾ pint (425ml) milk or soya milk
2 eggs

Slice the bananas and marinate in the fruit juice for at least half an hour.

Grease a 7" (18cm) oven dish with a little butter. Line the bottom of the dish with breadcrumbs, then make alternate layers of banana, breadcrumbs and brown sugar; finishing with a layer of crumbs.

Make up the juice to 1 pint (575ml) with milk and add the eggs. Beat together well. Pour over the crumb and banana mixture and leave to stand for at least an hour.

Bake at 350°F/180°C/Gas 4 for about ¾–1 hour until firm to the touch. Slice and serve with whipped cream.

Bande Napoleon

Serves 6

Food For Friends, Brighton
Chef; Bix Gatenby

For the pastry:

10 oz (275g) wholewheat pastry flour, sieved and the bran added back later
10 oz (275g) butter or kosher margarine
1 teaspoon salt
5 fl oz (150ml) water
2 teaspoons lemon juice

For the pastry cream:

½ pint (275ml) milk
3 egg yolks
3 oz (75g) sugar

1 drop vanilla essence
1½ oz (35g) wholewheat flour
a little kirsch

For the filling:

½ pint (275ml) double cream, whisked until stiff
4 oz (125g) fresh strawberries, hulled washed and dried
2 kiwi fruit, sliced
a little icing sugar, to finish

This simplest of concepts may give wholewheat flour the boost it needs to go marching into the 21st century with no worries about the competition. The dish is literally built; there are three phases and is a sandwich of the lightest wholewheat pastry, pastry cream and soft fresh fruit.

Make the pastry by placing the flour and salt in a bowl. Make a well in the centre and gradually add the water and lemon juice, mixing until a dough has formed. Knead until smooth. Cover and leave to rest for half an hour in the fridge.

Roll the dough into a rectangle. Divide the butter into four and then, taking one portion, dot small pieces of the butter all over the pastry rectangle. Draw the top two corners of the pastry over the centre and fold the remaining third of the pastry up to form an envelope. Lightly seal the edges with the rolling pin. Trim the pastry round once so that the largest seam is to your left. Repeat the rolling, dotting and folding process and then leave to rest in the fridge for at least 20 minutes.

Repeat the rolling and folding process with the two remaining butter portions. Refrigerate.

Moisten a 10 × 12 in (25 × 32cm) baking sheet. Roll the pastry out to the same size. Glaze the surface with egg wash (taking care not to allow it to run down the sides) and prick the surface over lightly with a fork. Leave to rest for 20 minutes and then bake at 425°F/220°C/Gas 7 for 25–30 minutes. Remove from the oven and allow to cool. Using a sharp knife cut into 3 equal sized oblongs.

Make the pastry cream by bringing the milk to the boil. Cream together the eggs, sugar and flour and vanilla. Pour the milk over and whisk briskly. Return to the saucepan and bring milk to the boil, stirring continuously. Cook for 2 minutes and remove from the heat and leave to cool. Add a little kirsch to flavour. If the cream is being stored for any length of time, cover it with buttered paper to prevent a skin forming.

For the filling, fold the strawberries and kiwi slices gently into the whipped cream.

To assemble the bande, take one layer of pastry and cover with the pastry cream, spreading it evenly and right to the edges. Cover with a second layer of pastry and top that with the cream mixture. Finally place the last pastry oblong on top and sprinkle it with the icing sugar. Flash the bande under a very hot grill or sear it with a hot poker.

Banoffi Pie

Richmond Harvest, Richmond
Head chef; Jenny Howell
Second chefs; Sandra Mahaney and Helene Shlamka

1 small packet wholewheat biscuits
3 oz (75g) melted margarine
1 tin (15 oz/425g) condensed milk, boiled in the tin for 2 hours, cooled
2 bananas sliced
7 fl oz (200ml) whipping cream
soft brown sugar to taste
instant coffee powder to taste
2 tablespoons natural yoghurt
3 oz (75g) walnuts, roughly chopped

Crush the biscuits and add the melted margarine, so that the crumbs are well coated. Press on to the base of a dish.

Spread the contents of the tin of condensed milk on top of the biscuit base and cover with banana slices.

Whip together the cream, sugar and coffee until the cream is stiff. Fold in the yoghurt.

Spread the cream on top of the bananas, smooth over the top and decorate with chopped walnuts.

Blackberry Crisp

Nature's Way, Eastbourne
Chefs; Maurice and Dorothy Fossitt

6 oz (175g) fresh wholemeal breadcrumbs
1½ lb (675g) blackberries, fresh or frozen and de-frosted
2 large bananas, thinly sliced
8 oz (225g) soft brown sugar
2 oz (50g) vegetable margarine
grated rind of 1 medium orange
juice from 2 medium oranges

Grease a 3 pint (1⅝ litre) dish.

Sprinkle 2 oz (50g) breadcrumbs over the bottom of the dish. Cover with the blackberries and banana slices and then sprinkle over the remaining crumbs.

Put the sugar, margarine, orange rind and juice in a saucepan and heat together gently until the sugar has dissolved.

Pour over the crumb mixture.

Bake in the centre of the oven at 400°F/200°C/Gas 6 for 30–40 minutes.

Serve hot or cold with cream.

Carob and Hazelnut Mousse

Serves 6

The Old Bakehouse, Castle Cary
Chef; Carol Seeley

4 oz (125g) ground hazelnuts
3 large eggs, separated
2 oz (50g) raw brown sugar
5 oz (150g) carob bar
3 oz (75g) softened margarine
1 tablespoon brandy

Beat the egg yolks with the sugar until pale and thick.

Melt the carob by placing in a bowl over a saucepan of simmering water.

Add the margarine and the melted carob to the egg yolk mixture.

Fold in the stiffly beaten egg whites and the hazelnuts. Finally stir in the brandy.

Serve in stemmed wine glasses with cream and a whole hazelnut to decorate. Very rich and delicious!

Cranks Raw Sugar Brulée

Serves 6

Cranks, London

6 egg yolks
4 tablespoons raw demerara sugar
½ teaspoon vanilla essence
1 pint (575ml) single cream
raw brown sugar to cover

One of the most delicious desserts ever . . . but plan it two days in advance!

Put the egg yolks, demerara sugar and vanilla into a bowl and beat until pale and thick. Place the cream in a saucepan and stir over the heat until it almost boils. Remove from the heat and add to the egg yolk mixture. Beat well with a wooden spoon until combined. Put the bowl over a pan of simmering water and stir until the mixture coats the back of a wooden spoon. Remove from the heat immediately. Strain into 6 individual heatproof dishes. Put the dishes into a baking tray and pour in enough boiling water to come halfway up the sides. Bake in the oven at 300°F/150°C/Gas 2 for about 30 minutes or until the custard has set lightly. Cool. Refrigerate overnight.

Sift the raw brown sugar and spoon over the custards in a thin even layer. Preheat the grill until very hot. Put the dishes of custard underneath and allow the sugar to melt and brown — be careful not to let it burn. Cool and refrigerate until ready to serve, when it will be deliciously crisp on top and creamy inside.

ALTERNATIVE: if wished the single cream may be infused with a flavouring before the custard is made. Leave out the vanilla and choose from — a fresh bay leaf, a sprig of fresh rosemary, a few pieces of chopped orange or lemon rind; or add a few drops of rose water or a few drops of orange flower water.

Reproduced from *Entertaining With Cranks,* by Kay Canter and Daphne Swann. Published by JM Dent & Sons Ltd.

Carrot and Coconut Cake

Serves 8–10

The Quarry Shop, Machynlleth
Chef; Anne Lowmass

6 fl oz (175ml) vegetable oil
3 eggs, beaten
1 teaspoon sea salt
7 oz (200g) wholemeal flour
1 tablespoon cinnamon
7 oz (200g) muscovado sugar
3 oz (75g) desiccated coconut
1½ teaspoons baking powder
1 large carrot, grated

A dark, moist cake which is delicious served as a sweet with cream or yoghurt.

Mix the oil, beaten eggs and salt together.

In a separate bowl combine the flour, cinnamon, sugar, coconut, baking powder and carrot, then mix the wet and dry ingredients. It is easier to add the wet ingredients to the dry. Stir well until you achieve a smooth consistency.

Pour into an 8" (20cm) square, oiled and lined cake tin. Bake for 35 minutes at 350°F/180°C/Gas 4 until the top is firm.

Carrot and Hazelnut Pudding

Serves 4

Wholemeal Café, London
Chef; Simon Wadmore

5 oz (150g) carrots, grated
2 oz (50g) dates, chopped
2 oz (50g) sultanas
2 oz (50g) raisins
4 oz (125g) roasted hazelnuts
4 tablespoons honey
4 oz (125g) butter, melted

Mix all the ingredients together well and bake at 350°F/180°C/Gas 4 for 30 minutes, in a small cake tin.

Serve hot with yoghurt or cream.

Chocolate, Banana and Rum Crisp

Serves 4

Saxon's, Brighton
Chef; Saxon Howard

2 bananas
2 measures dark rum
juice of ½ lemon
1 teaspoon ground ginger
4 oz (125g) muscovado sugar
2 oz (50g) cocoa powder
8 oz (225g) wholewheat breadcrumbs
½ cup cooking oil or 4 oz (125g) margarine

Alcohol has a habit of creeping into a lot of my recipes!

Slice the bananas finely and soak in the rum, lemon juice and ginger.

Mix the sugar and cocoa powder into the breadcrumbs, then rub in the oil or margarine.

Place half the banana mixture in the base of a small greased ovenproof dish, followed by half the breadcrumbs. Then add the remaining banana and finally a layer of breadcrumbs.

Cook at 350°F/180°C/Gas 4 for 25 minutes. Serve with cream or yoghurt.

Chocolate Coffee Trifle

Food For Thought, London
Chef; Kit Norman

6 oz (175g) margarine
4 oz (125g) demerara sugar
3 eggs
1 rounded teaspoon baking powder
6 oz (175g) wholewheat flour
3 drops vanilla essence
1 dessertspoon coffee and chicory essence
4 oz (125g) mixed sultanas and raisins soaked in 1 tablespoon rum
3 bananas, sliced
1 pint (575ml) prepared custard
2 oz (50g) dark chocolate, grated
1 lb (450g) demerara sugar
grated chocolate, for garnish

Cream margarine and sugar until fluffy, beat in the eggs one at a time and then fold in the sifted flour and baking powder.

Add the vanilla and coffee essences, and if necessary add a little milk to achieve a smooth mixture.

Spread the mixture into a greased sandwich tin and bake at 300°F/150°C/Gas 2 for 25–30 minutes. Cool and cut into bite-sized squares.

Place the sponge pieces in a large, shallow serving dish and cover with raisins, sultanas and sliced bananas.

Make up the custard and before removing from the heat add the chocolate and sugar. Stir in until they have dissolved and are distributed evenly throughout the custard. Leave to cool.

Pour the custard over the sponge. When set sprinkle with grated chocolate and serve with whipped cream.

Coconut Flapjack

Hannah's, Worthing

8 oz (225g) margarine
8 oz (225g) brown sugar
4 oz (125g) sultanas
8 oz (225g) syrup
8 oz (225g) coconut, desiccated
8 oz (225g) oats

Put the margarine, brown sugar, sultanas and syrup in a large saucepan and heat together gently until the sugar has dissolved and the syrup and margarine have melted.

Remove from the heat, stir in the coconut and then the oats, mixing well to make sure the ingredients are evenly distributed.

Pour into a greased swiss roll tin and bake for 40 minutes at 350°F/180°C/Gas 4.

Remove from the oven and leave to set before cutting into squares or fingers. The mixture should still have a slightly sticky texture.

Chocolate, Orange and Apricot Pudding

Delany's, Shrewsbury

For the fruit filling:

3 oranges
4 oz (125g) dried apricots
5 fl oz (150ml) orange juice

For the sponge:

6 oz (175g) margarine or butter
6 oz (175g) dark muscovado sugar
3 eggs
6 oz (175g) wholemeal flour
3 teaspoons baking powder
4–5 heaped teaspoons cocoa powder
½ teaspoon ground mace
2 tablespoons natural yoghurt

For the topping:

2 tablespoons honey
rind of 1 orange

This is delicious served with natural yoghurt or whipped cream and can be eaten hot or cold. The yoghurt can easily be substituted for rum in the sponge mixture to give an even richer taste.

Prepare the fruit filling. Ring the 3 oranges and keep the rind for the sponge. Remove all the skin and pith from the oranges and then segment them. Place in a 2 pint (1.1 litre) ovenproof dish.

Chop the apricots in half and gently cook them in a pan with just enough orange juice to cover them. Once soft strain the apricots and place them on top of the orange segments.

Make the sponge. Beat together the margarine and sugar until light and fluffy (preferably in a food processor).

Add the three eggs and continue beating until they are evenly distributed and the mixture has become a liquid. Fold in the flour, baking powder, cocoa powder and mace. Mix in the yoghurt and the rind from the three oranges.

Pour the sponge mixture over the fruit and bake at 350°F/180°C/Gas 4 for about 50 minutes, or until the centre feels spongy to the touch.

Remove the sponge from the oven and glaze with the mixture of the orange rind mixed into the melted honey and then brushed over the top of the sponge.

Chocolate Roulade

Gannets, Newark
Chef; Hilary Bower

6 medium eggs, separated
7 oz (200g) caster sugar
2 oz (50g) cocoa
5 oz (150g) Bournville chocolate
½ pint (275ml) double cream, whipped

Grease a Swiss roll tin approximately 13 × 8 × 1" (32.3 × 20 × 2.5cm). Line the tin with Bakewell paper, making sure the corners fit well.

Whisk the egg yolks in a bowl until thickened. Add the sugar and beat again until thick but not white. Add the cocoa and mix well.

Whisk the egg whites until stiff but not dry and fold carefully into the cocoa mixture.

Put the mixture into the prepared tin making sure it is spread evenly. Bake at 350°F/180°C/Gas 4 for 20 minutes. When cooked the sponge should be set, but not dry. This is very important, as a dry sponge will crack badly when you try to roll it.

Leave the sponge to cool in the tin, and then turn it out on to a sheet of greaseproof paper generously dusted with caster sugar.

Melt the chocolate with 2 tablespoons water in a basin, over hot water. Remove the basin from the pan and allow to cool slightly, stirring occasionally. Spread the chocolate over the sponge, and then cover with two thirds of the whipped cream.

Using the greaseproof paper to help, carefully roll up the sponge. Transfer to a large serving dish. Decorate the top of the roulade with the remaining cream, and if desired, add a little grated chocolate.

Marbled Chocolate Cheesecake

Pilgrims, Tunbridge Wells
Chef; Margaret Stanbury

8 oz (225g) chocolate flavoured biscuits, crushed finely
2 oz (50g) coffee flavoured biscuits, crushed finely
½ teaspoon ground cinnamon
5 oz (150g) butter, melted
1½ lb (700g) cream cheese, softened
8 oz (225g) caster sugar
3 eggs, beaten
4 fl oz (125ml) cream
1 teaspoon brandy or rum essence
6 oz (175g) pure cooking chocolate, melted
whipped cream, for decoration

Combine the crushed biscuits with the cinnamon and melted butter. Mix thoroughly and press on to the base and sides of a well greased 9" (23cm) spring form tin. Chill for 30 minutes.

Preheat the oven to 300°F/150°C/Gas 2. Beat the cream cheese in a large bowl until softened. Gradually add the sugar, then the beaten eggs, mixing well after each addition. Stir in the cream and essence. Spoon all but 1 cup of the mixture into the crumb crust.

Combine the remaining mixture with the warm melted chocolate and drizzle this over the plain mixture with a thin bladed knife or skewer. Swirl the chocolate through the plain mixture to create a marbled effect.

Bake for 35–40 minutes. Open the oven door after this time and leave the cheesecake in the oven until cold.

Chill for several hours then decorate with whipped cream.

Yorkshire Curd Tart

Serves 4–6

York Wholefood, York
Chef; Christine Worrallo

7" (18cm) flan ring lined with shortcrust pastry
3 tablespoons lemon curd or raspberry jam (lemon curd gives a better flavour)
8 oz (225g) curd cheese
2 oz (50g) currants
pinch of nutmeg
1 egg, beaten
1 oz (25g) butter, melted

If you can obtain curds which have been allowed to set naturally, rather than being set with vinegar, the tart will have a much softer texture.

Pour the warmed lemon curd or jam over the pastry base.

Mash the curd cheese, then add the currants, nutmeg, egg and butter. Mix well.

Fill the flan case and bake at 400°F/200°C/Gas 6 for 20–30 minutes, until golden brown.

Figs in Rum

Cherry Orchard, London
Chef; Trish Mander

1 lb (450g) dried figs
juice of 1 lemon
2 oz (50g) currants
2 fl oz (50ml) rum
1 dessertspoon honey or golden syrup
½ teaspoon mixed spice
1 dessertspoon cornflour

It started off as a fig pie, didn't feel like making pastry and then needed that little something . . .

Place the figs in a saucepan and add the lemon juice and enough water to cover them by an inch (2.5cm). Stew for half an hour.

Strain the figs, retaining the liquid.

Leave the figs to cool in a bowl with the currants and half the rum.

Make the sauce. Add the honey and spice to the fig water and heat.

Whilst the liquid is heating take a little of it from the pan and mix with the cornflour to form a smooth, thin paste. Return this paste to the pan and stir continually until the sauce thickens.

Add the rest of the rum to the sauce and pour over the figs. Allow to stand until cool and then place in the fridge to chill. Serve with cream or ice cream or as a special treat, with soured cream.

Fruit Nut Gateau

Rainbows End Café, Glastonbury
Chef; Shelagh Spear

For the base:

3 eggs
6 oz (175g) soft light brown sugar
8 oz (225g) mixed ground nuts, e.g. brazils, walnuts and hazelnuts

For the decoration:

½ pint (275ml) whipping cream
Fresh fruit to decorate e.g. nectarines, black grapes, kiwi fruit and cherries,
   mint or strawberry leaves.

I developed this recipe to make the most of the spectacular selection of fruits now available to us. The fresh fruit decoration provides a mixture of colours and taste. Any fresh fruits can be used: whatever is in season. The nut "macaroon" base uses no flour and is therefore useful for gluten and wheat free diets.

Whisk the whole eggs to a stiff foam.

Add the sugar and whisk until well mixed.

Fold in the finely ground nuts.

Prepare an 8" (20cm) loose bottomed metal quiche tray. Line it with foil then brush with oil. Pour in the nut and egg mixture and place in an oven at 375°F/190°C/Gas 5. After 30 minutes turn the oven temperature down to 325°F/170°C/Gas 3 and continue to cook for a further 15 minutes. Remove from the oven and leave in the tin until cold. Once cold remove from the tin, peel back the foil carefully and place on a serving plate or cake stand.

Spread the base with whipped cream.

Stud the top with circles of fresh fruit and leaves. If preferred all of one fruit can be used, e.g. strawberries or grapes.

Fruit Snow

Harvest Vegetarian, Ambleside
Chef; Gillian Kelly

1 lb (450g) mixed dried fruit; e.g. sultanas, currants, raisins, chopped dates,
    chopped figs, chopped dried apricots, peaches, pears and apples or dried
    tropical fruits
2 baking apples, peeled and diced (optional)
2 bananas
2 oz (50g) desiccated coconut
cream or yoghurt, to serve

Soak the dried fruit for at least two hours, and preferably overnight.

Put the fruit in a pan with the soaking liquid and bring to the boil. Lower the heat and
cook gently for 15 minutes. Add the apples if you are using them and continue cooking
for a further 15 minutes or until all the fruit is soft. Add more water as necessary; the
mixture should be thick and juicy but not in danger of sticking to the pan.

Remove from the heat and allow to cool. Slice the bananas into the cooked fruit, put
the mixture in a serving dish and top with a layer of desiccated coconut. Chill
thoroughly before serving on its own or with cream or yoghurt.

Guinness Loaf

Guild Café, Bristol

1 ½ lb (900g) mixed dried fruit
½ pint (275ml) Guinness
8 oz (225g) dark brown sugar
4 oz (125g) chopped walnuts
1 large egg (beaten with a tablespoon milk)
1 lb (450g) 81% wholemeal flour (or similar)
2 ½ level teaspoons baking powder

It is worth making two loaves at once as they keep well in an airtight tin for a couple of weeks and indeed taste even better after the first few days.

Soak the fruit in the Guinness overnight.

Preheat the oven to 325°F/170°C/Gas Mark 3.

Add all the remaining ingredients to the fruit and stir until smooth. If the mixture seems too dry add a little more milk.

Divide the mixture between two large, greased, loaf tins and bake in the centre of the oven for 1 ½ hours or until springy to the touch. Turn on to a rack to cool.

Serve cut into slices, and to make it even more delicious, spread with butter.

Honey Shoofly Pie

Good Earth, Wells
Chef; Tina Dearling

Pastry:

6 oz (175g) 81% wholemeal flour
3 oz (75g) margarine
water to mix

Filling:

2 oz (50g) butter
2 oz (50g) light muscovado sugar
2 teaspoons lemon juice
4 oz (125g) wholewheat breadcrumbs

Make the pastry. Rub the margarine into the flour. Add enough water to form a workable dough. Roll out on to a floured board and line an 8" (20 cm) flan dish. Save any remaining pastry.

Make the filling. Melt the butter in a pan. Add sugar, honey and lemon juice. Heat until the mixture turns runny then add the breadcrumbs and stir in well.

Spread the breadcrumb mixture into the flan case. Cut any remaining pastry into thin strips and arrange on the top of the flan in a criss-cross pattern. Bake at 350°F/180°C/Gas 4 for about 30 minutes or until the pastry is golden. Serve with cream or custard.

Melon Mousse

Wild Oats II, Bristol
Chef; Loes Abrahams

1 large melon
1 bottle natural unfiltered apple juice
agar agar flakes
2 oz (50g) roasted and chopped hazelnuts

Remove the seeds from the melon, scoop out the flesh and place in a blender. Blend well.

Place the apple juice in a saucepan and add to it 1 tablespoon of agar agar flakes for each pint of juice. Heat gently until the agar agar has dissolved and allow to cool slightly.

Add the juice to the melon, blend again and pour the mixture into a glass bowl. Leave to set.

Just before serving garnish with hazelnuts.

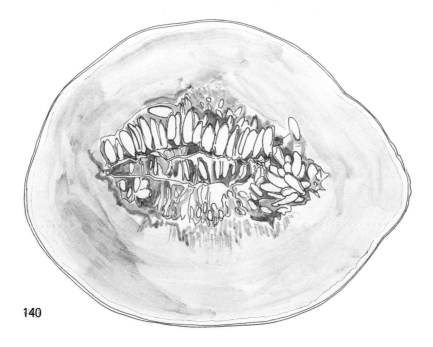

Norwegian Cream

Dumb Waiter Bistro, Todmorden
Chef; Jeffrey Taylor

2 egg yolks
2 whole eggs
1 teaspoon vanilla essence
2 oz (50g) caster sugar
¾ pint (400ml) milk
5 fl oz (150ml) cream
8 oz (225g) dried apricots, cooked and puréed

For the decoration:

whipped cream
grated chocolate

Beat the egg yolks and whole eggs together with the vanilla essence and caster sugar until well mixed.

Bring the milk to the boil, then pour on to the egg mixture, stirring well and finally add the cream.

Pour ¾ of this mixture into a 2 pint (generous litre) pyrex dish and cook in a bain marie at 325°F/170°C/Gas 3 until just set.

Heat the apricot purée through and carefuly spoon it on to the cooked cream, forming an even layer. Pour over the remaining ¼ of the cream and return to the oven to finish cooking. The top of the custard should be set and slightly firm to the touch. The entire cooking time will be about 1½ hours.

Remove from the oven and leave to go completely cold. Pipe the top with whipped cream and sprinkle over grated chocolate.

Dairy Free Orange Cake

Herbs, Skipton
Chef; Joan Fikkert

8 oz (225g) vegetable margarine
8 oz (225g) demerara sugar
1 lb (450g) self-raising wholemeal flour
2 teaspoons mixed spice
8 oz (225g) sultanas
grated rind of 2 oranges
½ pint (275ml) fresh orange juice

Although initially baked for our vegan customers, it has become a favourite with everyone.

Beat the margarine and sugar together until pale in appearance.

Mix the flour, spice, sultanas and orange rind together.

Put the orange juice into a pan and bring to the boil. Cool slightly, then gradually mix into the flour.

Stir the flour mixture into the creamed margarine and sugar and mix well.

Put the mixture into a 10" (25cm) loose bottomed tin which has been greased and lined. Bake at 300°F/150°C/Gas 2 for about 1¼ hours. This makes quite a dry mixture, so take care when turning it out, it is crumbly.

Pear and White Wine Fool

Huckleberry's, Bath
Chef; Vicky Cox

6 pears, peeled, quartered and cored
3 tablespoons honey
½ teaspoon ground cinnamon
¼ cup white wine
3 teaspoons agar agar
1 pint (575ml) natural yoghurt

Stew the pears in the wine, honey and cinnamon until soft. Add the agar agar and heat gently until it has melted.

Blend the pear mixture with the yoghurt, pour into a serving dish and chill for 1–2 hours until firm.

Poached Pears in Port with Blackberry Sauce and Brandy Snaps

Food For Thought, London
Chef; Siriporn Duncan

2 ripe pears
2 fl oz (50ml) port
1 lb (450g) blackberries
2 oz (50g) caster sugar

Peel the pears and place in a heavy saucepan with the port.

Cover and poach very gently for 5 minutes, turning pears once.

When tender, chill and then cut the pears in two lengthways discarding the pips. Then cut the halves into 5–6 thin slices.

To make the sauce, place the blackberries and the sugar in a heavy saucepan, cover, and cook gently until tender. Rub blackberries through a sieve and chill the resulting purée.

For the brandy snaps:

1 oz (25g) demerara sugar
1 oz (25g) butter
1 oz (25g) golden syrup
1 oz (25g) plain flour
1 teaspoon lemon juice
whipped cream flavoured with brandy

Melt the sugar, butter and syrup together in a saucepan and then add the warmed flour and lemon juice. Stir well.

Put teaspoonfuls of the mixture on to well greased baking trays leaving 6" (15cm) between spoonfuls to allow for spreading.

Bake at 350°F/180°C/Gas 4 until golden brown. Remove from the oven, leave to cool for just a few seconds and then lift each snap off the tray one at a time and wrap it around the greased handle of a wooden spoon. It should go crisp in just a few minutes. It may help to have several baking trays and spoons at the ready so that you can work a production line.

Once all the brandy snaps are cold fill them with whipped cream. Try to serve them within an hour of filling otherwise they may go soft.

Pecan Pie

Herbs, Coventry
Chef; Robert Jackson

For the pastry:

8 oz (225g) plain wholemeal flour
4 oz (125g) butter or margarine
1 egg, beaten
a little water

For the filling:

3 eggs
4 oz (125g) soft brown sugar
1 teaspoon vanilla essence
3 oz (75g) butter, melted
3 tablespoons golden syrup
3 tablespoons honey
8 oz (225g) shelled pecan nuts, chopped – reserve a few whole for decoration

This wonderful creation can be eaten hot or cold and although the pecan nuts may seem a bit of an extravagance, they are worth every penny!

To prepare the base, rub the fat into the flour to resemble fine breadcrumbs. Add sufficient egg and water to make a smooth dough. Roll out and use to line a 9" (23cm) flan ring or sandwich tin. Prick the base over, place a piece of greaseproof paper lightly in the centre and pour over some baking beans. Bake in a pre-heated oven at 375°F/190°C/Gas 5 for about 10 minutes. Leave to cool slightly and remove greaseproof paper.

Make the filling. Lightly beat the eggs, beat in the sugar, vanilla essence, butter, syrup and honey and stir in the chopped pecans.

Pour into the partially baked pastry case and decorate the top with the reserved pecans.

Bake for approximately 30–40 minutes, still at 375°F/190°C/Gas 5, until golden brown and firm. Leave to cool slightly.

For a special finish, heat together 2 tablespoons apricot jam with 2 tablespoons water until the jam is completely melted. Cool slightly and then brush the top of the pie with the glaze. Serve either hot or cold with whipped cream, vanilla ice cream or yoghurt.

Raspberry and Kiwi Meringue

Arnolfini, Bristol

6 egg whites
12 oz (350g) caster sugar
15 oz (425g) tin of raspberries (or 1 lb (450g) of fresh raspberries)
3 kiwi fruit
1 pint (575ml) whipping cream

Whisk the egg whites until stiff, and fold in the sugar.

Line a baking tray with greaseproof paper. Spread the meringue mixture evenly over the tray and bake in a low oven 110°C/200°F/Gas ¼ until crisp – 2–3 hours.

Leave the meringue to cool, then crumble it up roughly.

Whip the cream. Peel and finely slice the kiwi fruit and wash and hull the raspberries. Layer all the ingredients in a serving dish, alternating the colours. Decorate the final layer with a combination of kiwi fruit and raspberries.

Redcurrant Meringue Pie

Serves 6

Good Earth, Wells
Chef; Tina Dearling

For the pastry:

5 oz (150g) margarine or butter
4 oz (125g) caster sugar
4 egg yolks
3 oz (75g) ground almonds
9 oz (250g) plain flour

For the filling:

4 egg whites
8 oz (225g) caster sugar
1 lb (450g) raw redcurrants
2 oz (50g) caster sugar

Make the pastry. Mix all the ingredients to a dough in a food processor. Roll out to line a 9" (23cm) flan tin. Leave to rest then bake until golden brown at 375°F/190°C/Gas 5.

Mix the redcurrants with the 2 oz (50g) sugar and then place in the flan case.

Make the meringue by whisking the egg whites until stiff, then add 4 oz (125g) sugar, whisk again until stiff, and finally fold in the remaining 4 oz (125g) sugar. Pile the meringue on to the fruit, making sure you take it right to the pastry to completely cover the fruit.

Cook until the meringue is a little coloured and the fruit just cooked at 425°F/220°C/Gas 7. Serve warm or chilled.

Rum Crackle

Lakeland Hedgerow, Bowness on Windermere
Chefs; Jennifer Mason, Stephen Davy

2 oz (50g) demerara sugar
2 oz (50g) butter
2 oz (50g) golden syrup
2 oz (50g) plain flour
1 tablespoon lemon juice
½ teaspoon ground ginger

Set the oven to 375°F/190°C/Gas 5.

Grease 2 or 3 baking sheets and one end of a wide rolling pin.

Melt the sugar, butter and syrup together. Remove from the heat, sift in the flour and then stir in the lemon juice and ginger making sure they are mixed in well.

Place teaspoonfuls of mixture on to the baking trays, about 6" (15cm) apart to allow for spreading. Bake for 5–7 minutes until golden brown.

Allow to cool for a few seconds and then carefully remove from the baking tray with a palette knife. Quickly shape round the rolling pin to form a "U" shape and leave for a few seconds to harden slightly. Then remove from the pin and place on a wire rack to cool completely. It may help to have several trays and more than one rolling pin if you can to maintain a continuous production line.

For the caramel sauce:

3 oz (75g) granulated sugar
7 fl oz (200ml) water

Place 2 oz (50g) sugar in a pan and melt slowly until brown and bubbly.

Add the water, stir well and then add the remaining sugar. Reboil, stirring all the time, and cook until the mixture is of a syrup consistency. Allow to cool.

For the rum cream:

½ pint (275ml) double cream
rum to taste

Whip the cream until firm then add rum to taste.

To assemble:

the crackle "boats"
20—24 kumquats
rum cream
caramel sauce

Fill the centre of each boat with 3—4 kumquats.

Pipe the rum cream into each end of the boats, filling them completely.

Spoon the caramel sauce down the length of each boat.

Serve immediately. Orange segments can be used instead of kumquats if desired but the overall effect is not quite so attractive.

Strawberry and Honey Ice Cream
Serves 4

Cheese Press, Crickhowell
Chef; Mrs Morgan Grenville

1 ½ tablespoons runny honey
6 oz (175g) fresh strawberries
5 fl oz (150ml) whipped cream
1 egg white

Blend the honey and strawberries together in a liquidizer or food processor. (Or pass the strawberries through a sieve and then mix with the honey.)

Stir in the whipped cream and place in the freezer until just frozen.

Whisk the egg white stiffly and fold into the ice cream, making sure there are no white lumps showing.

Freeze again for several hours, or preferably overnight, then serve. The ice cream can be frozen in any freezer proof container, but you will find it will freeze faster in metal.

Llanwrtyd Baked Trifle

Cnapan, Newport
Chef; Eluned Lloyd

2 jam swiss rolls
brandy, to taste
1 tin of apricots or pears, sliced
2 whole eggs
2 egg yolks
¾ pint (425ml) milk
sugar, to taste

Line a large pudding basin with thin slices of swiss roll, tightly packed. Soak with brandy.

Drain the fruit and layer it alternately with swiss roll. Marinate the swiss roll with brandy as you go and make sure you finish with a layer of swiss roll.

Make a custard. Beat the eggs and egg yolks together with the milk and sugar. Heat very gently without bringing to the boil and stirring all the time, until the custard thickens slightly.

Using a skewer make small holes through the layers of swiss roll and fruit. Carefully pour the thin custard over the sponge. It should gradually all be absorbed. Cover with greaseproof paper and then foil.

Steam or cook in a slow cooker for 3½ hours. Chill well before serving. Serve with cream or yoghurt.

Water Chestnut Pudding

Cook's Delight, Berkhamsted
Chef; Khaieng Tyler

6 oz (175g) tin water chestnuts
1 teaspoon roasted sesame oil
½ pint (275ml) water
4 tablespoons kuzu or arrowroot
4 tablespoons rice syrup

Grate the water chestnuts. Fry in the sesame oil. Add most of the water to the fried chestnuts, leaving enough to dissolve the kuzu in a suribachi.

Stir the dissolved kuzu into the water chestnuts. Add the rice syrup and cook until the ingredients have blended. Pour into a serving dish and leave to cool.

Notes

Notes

Addresses

Arnolfini	— Narrow Quay, Bristol	0272 299191
Cheese Press	— 18 High St., Crickhowell	0873 811122
Cherry Orchard	— 241 Globe Rd., London E2	01-985 0641
Clinchs Salad House	— 14 Southgate, Chichester	0243 788822
Cnapan	— East St., Newport, Dyfed	0239 820575
Cooks Delight	— 360–362 High St., Berkhamsted	04427 3584
Cranks	— 8 Marshall St., London W1	01-437 9431
Delany's	— St. Julian's Craft Centre, Shrewsbury	0743 60602
Dumb Waiter	— 23 Water St., Todmorden	070-681 5387
Everyman Bistro	— 9 Hope Street, Liverpool	051-708 9545
Food For Friends	— 17a–18 Prince Albert St., Brighton	0273 202310
Food For Health	— 15/17 Blackfriars Lane, London EC4	01-236 7001
Food For Thought	— 31 Neal St., Covent Garden, London WC2	01-836 0239
Gannets	— 35 Castlegate, Newark	0636 702066
Good Earth	— 4 Priory Rd., Wells	0749 78600
Guild Café	— 66–70 Park St., Bristol	0272 25548
Hannah	— 165 Montague St., Worthing	0903 31132
Harvest	— Compston Rd., Ambleside	09663 3151
Henderson's Salad Table	— 94 Hanover St., Edinburgh	031-225 3400
Herbs	— 28 Lower Holyhead Rd., Coventry	0203 555654
Herbs	— 10 High St., Skipton	0756 60619
Hockneys	— 96/98 High St., Croydon	01-688 2899
Huckleberry's	— 34 Broad St., Bath	0225 64876
Lakeland Hedgerow	— Greenbank, Bowness on Windermere	096 62 5002
Marno's	— 14 St. Nicholas St., Ipswich	0473 53106
Nature's Way	— 198 Terminus Rd., Eastbourne	0323 643211
Neal's Yard	— 6 Neal's Yard, London WC2	01-836 5199
Nuthouse	— 26 Kingly St., London W1	01-437 9471
Old Bakehouse	— High St., Castle Cary	0963 50067
Pilgrims	— 37 Mount Ephraim, Tunbridge Wells	0892 20341
Rainbows End	— 17a High St., Glastonbury	0458 33896
Richmond Harvest	— The Quadrant, Richmond	01-940 1138
Saxon's	— 48 George St., Brighton	0903 31132
Siop Y Chwarel (The Quarry Shop)	— 13 Heol Maengwyn, Machynlleth, Powys	0654 2624
Sree Krishna	— 194 Tooting High St., London SW17	01-672 4250
That Café	— 1031 Stockport Rd., Levenshulme, Manchester	061-432 4672
Wild Oats	— 11 Lower Redland Rd., Bristol	0272 731967
Wholemeal Café	— 1 Shrubbery Rd., Streatham, London SW16	01-769 2423
York Wholefood	— 98 Micklegate, York	0904 56804

Index